Tales of Lights and Shadows

Also available from *Continuum:*

Myth: Key Concepts in Religion, Robert Ellwood
Tales of Darkness, Robert Ellwood

Tales of Lights and Shadows

Mythology of the Afterlife

Robert Ellwood

continuum

Continuum International Publishing Group

The Tower Building	80 Maiden Lane
11 York Road	Suite 704
London SE1 7NX	New York NY 10038

www.continuumbooks.com

British Library Cataloguing-in-Publication Data
A catalogue record for this book is available from the British Library.

ISBN: HB: 978-1-4411-7003-3
      PB: 978-1-4411-4397-6

Library of Congress Cataloging-in-Publication Data
Ellwood, Robert S., 1933–
    Tales of lights and shadows : mythology of the afterlife / Robert Ellwood.
        p. cm.
    ISBN 978–1–4411–4397–6—ISBN 978–1–4411–7003–3   1. Future life.
2. Mythology.   I. Title.   II. Series.
BL535.E66 2010
202'.3—dc22   2010002076

Typeset by RefineCatch Limited, Bungay, Suffolk
Printed and bound in   India by Replika Press Pvt Ltd

Contents

Chapter 1

In That Good Night, What Dreams May Come? Myth, Meaning, and Afterlife

Do not go gentle into that good night
Dylan Thomas

For in that sleep of death what dreams may come,
When we have shuffled off this mortal coil
William Shakespeare

The Clear Light and the Smokey Path

You are a traditional Buddhist in Tibet. The hour of death has come upon you. Your body lies limp. You know that whatever in that frame was *you* is even now slipping away from its weight of flesh. The physical relics that remain will be taken to the charnel field where beasts and birds of prey will maul and devour them, for they no longer are of any human use. And yet, to feed even such carnivorous creatures as they is compassion, the religion's highest virtue.

As for yourself, as earthlight fades you hear, faintly but sufficiently, words whispered, almost chanted, into your ear, words in the voice of the lama attending you as you make this transition on the great pilgrimage. They are your instructions, your tour guidebook, so that nothing which confronts you will totally surprise you as a grand new adventure under a new sun unfolds. You will, in principle, be told in time how to respond to the many strange phenomena that are about to dazzle your eyes.

The darkness deepens, then suddenly light outbursts, light of a golden purity and power never seen on earth, the light of a thousand suns. And with it sounds the roaring of a thousand waterfalls at once. This is, the whisper tells you, the Clear Light of the Void, the very essence of the vast universe, the sound and sight of the dance of the galaxies and atoms distilled into a concentrate of unimaginable force.

Yet, you are told, that massive power is your own true nature, for you are and have always been as much a part of the dance as the remotest galaxy in the depths of space and time. Join it, let go to become part of it, and you are free, your pilgrimage having reached its ultimate goal, oneness with the One.

Yet you are not ready for this. You have not, in your time on earth, made enough deep meditations, moving consciousness beyond all name and form so that the one undifferentiated light seems familiar as family to you. If you had, you could now enter that supreme Reality as though returning to your own hearth and home. But as it is, the light is too bright for your eyes, feeling more like daggers than rays. The sound is too loud for your ears, drowning out even your own thoughts. You instinctively shrink back, and the magic moment when you might have gone where you most truly belong is gone. You see the ultimate light a little longer, as a dimmer and more distant radiant ring of eternity, but still you are too dazed by this strange new world to swim toward it. The secondary light too finally fades, leaving empty sky.

Not for long. Suddenly, as though a projector were switching slides, a vast and intricate figure looms above you amid the blue-black of infinite space. He is robed and crowned in white, he sits on a lion-throne and holds an eight-spoked wheel in his hand; he also holds in ecstatic sexual embrace his female consort. Radiant brilliance issues from his heart and that of the consort, so forcefully it is hard for your eyes to focus. We are now in the intermediate or Bardo state, the level of God or gods in heaven as it were, between God or Buddha-nature as infinite Clear Light, and the hard earth of our mortal lives.

The patter of words drones on, now telling you this is Vairocana, the cosmic Buddha whose meditations sustain the universe, who represents the Clear Light of the Void insofar as it can be represented in human form; his consort is Mother of Infinite Space, the profound wisdom with which he, as unlimited strength and skill, unites to manifest a universe. You realize that if you can truly recognize him as your own true nature, you will not fear but join him, entering his aura. You could do so if you had visualized him through meditation in the Tibetan style till you knew him as well as hands and feet. But again you are not prepared, and you pull back; the light again is too bright for your eyes. You are drawn to a softer white light off to one side of the vast phenomenon, and you are tempted to pursue it.

However, for the time being you stay with the passing panorama in the sky, as you see Vairocana fade out and another no less magnificent appear, and then another and another. These are the five cosmic

Buddhas of the great mandala or circle of power, who represent the immense forces and subtle layers of cosmic consciousness driving the universe itself. They appear in forms suitable for interface with human consciousness, as Buddhas in meditation so deep they uphold aspects of reality itself. Each holds his own symbol and embraces his own wisdom-queen. Yet they are all within each of us, for we are part of that reality, born from its mind and body, and able to return to it. If we recognize ourselves in any of the cosmic Buddhas, we can attain liberation through that gateway to infinity. You see them individually over five days, then on the sixth all five together, and on the seventh all five with attendant bodhisattvas.

The Buddha of the western wing of the mandala, Amitabha (Amida in Japanese), is particularly popular in East Asia, for it is said he has promised that all who call upon his name will be brought into his vast aura, which to our sight focuses as a Pure Land or Western Paradise, a virtually endless wonderland of gardens, trees strewn with nets of fabulous jewels, the music of paradise in the air.

Yet near each of the bright figures a dim light, in various colors, leads the overburdened eye away from the brilliant figure. These side-rays are six in number, tunneling toward six lokas or places of reincarnation. Those unable to receive the sublime images will find themselves especially drawn to one or another of those seductive pathways as a way of escape, because they correspond to the fate one's karma, or actions in thought, word, or deed, has prepared.

The white light leads to the heaven of the gods, the best karmic fate for those unprepared by spiritual meditation to receive Clear Light or the cosmic Buddhas; these happy fields are given those with a preponderance of good deeds in life. Then a soft red light will guide the wanderer between worlds to the realm of the asuras or fighting, jealous titans, the natural home of those who live by anger and violence. A soft blue light leads to human rebirth, with all its ambiguities. A soft green light takes us to the world of animals, said in Buddhist lore to be governed by sufferings and appetites which the creatures have no intelligence to understand; it draws those who, despite intelligence, have allowed their own lives to be guided mostly by appetite and suffering.

A soft yellow light leads to the realm of the hungry ghosts, creatures consumed by immense greed. Finally, a soft smoky light-trail takes one down deep to the dismal depths of hell. As in many religions, traditional commentators describe the imaginative tortures inflicted on the unfortunates consigned to hell with a certain relish. The main point, though, is that hell-beings really send themselves to this dark kingdom, by means of the state they have allowed their consciousnesses to reach: seeing themselves as entirely separate from all others, they inflict pain without compunction; here it is merely reflected back on themselves.

You may be drawn to follow down one of these light-paths, and will remain in it; not forever, but only as long as the karma you have generated keeps you there. When that energy is exhausted, you may revert back to the human realm, the only level at which you have mind and ability to make real choices, which in turn will determine your next destiny. But if you enter into the Clear Light or merge into one of the Buddhas, that is eternal ... unless you willingly return as a bodhisattva out of compassion for sentient beings.

Staying in the realm of Buddhic manifestations, continuing the heavenly panorama, you next see the five Buddhas in their terrifying aspects, as though your rejection of them has now turned them wrathful, or rather you perceive them as wrathful because of their threat to the separate individuality to which you still cling. But in your case, even the shock-therapy administered by their bloodthirsty horror is not enough to shake you free of self-clinging.

This is of great psychological interest, but we must proceed to the last stage of this scenario: since you did not find liberation in the intermediate state, you must now proceed to rebirth. You find yourself in a place of storm and tumbling rocks as the winds of karma blow stronger and stronger; you are told to pray to your patron deity, you have a flash vision of your future parents in sexual intercourse, you then faint and forget consciously all that has transpired, and find yourself in the womb of whatever creature, in whatever realm, your karma has scripted for you. In due course you are born, whether as human or dog, god or hungry ghost.

This is, as many will recognize, the after-death experience as portrayed in the text known to the west as *The Tibetan Book of the Dead*.[1] For the purposes of the present study, it can be considered a myth, since it presents important information about the human situation, its meaning and destiny, in story form: the story of 'you' as you pass through physical death, transit the 'in between' (Bardo) state, and enter rebirth.

Knowledge as Story, Story as Knowledge

Why story form? The issues of life, death, and afterlife have of course been dealt with more abstractly, in texts ranging from religious catechisms to recondite philosophy. But we are likely to find ourselves most engaged by *stories*, whether we believe them literally or not. That is, first of all, because our *lives* are stories, not abstractions. We are not just one thing, whether soul, mind, spirit, or flesh, nor just one kind of person, good or bad, but a long narrative in which now one, now another of our facets holds center stage, though the others are there, in the shadows or waiting in the wings:

> All the world's a stage,
>> And all the men and women merely players:
>> They have their exits and their entrances;
>> And one man in his time plays many parts . . .
>>   – Shakespeare, *As You Like It*, II, vii.

Second, not only are our lives stories, but – perhaps for that reason – we remember stories best. The roots of myth go back to preliterate times, when important information had to be conveyed from one generation to the next by word-of-mouth, through the lips of bards and elders who knew well what people needed to know. The data included knowledge of where the world, humanity, and one's own particular tribe had come from, on the grounds that to know thoroughly the nature of anything, one must know its origins. The wisdom included also the society's highest values, as exemplified by its heroes, its governance, its structure, its attitudes toward gods, animals, and tribal neighbors. And it also included knowledge about death, the spirits of the departed, and the likely experience of those who make that last long journey.

The loremasters who kept custody of this wisdom quickly realized it was imparted best through song and story, ideally the two combined in great epics. The first Australians learned the geography of their vast land through singing lengthy songs that recounted how tribal totem-ancestors created the features of that terrain back in the Dreamtime. Today, tribesmen walking those ancient 'songlines' and singing their songs of long ago can find their way, at the same time establishing a profoundly meaningful and sacred connection with the land.

Often a mythic story involves tension and action, for as every novelist knows, basic to any gripping narrative is a protagonist, the 'point of view' character, and an adversary or obstacle she or he must overcome. As the thrill of the drama holds us we also learn whatever information the story imparts along the way, often in the tale's very words. The storyteller too, in the days before writing, relied on the intense engagement lent by excitement, together with such devices as meter, rhyme, and stock phrases (all very evident in such epics as Homer's), to aid memorization.[2]

Clearly, a journey beyond death such as that narrated in *The Tibetan Book of the Dead* contains these features. It is a *vademecum*, a guide-book that can 'go with me,' literally as it is whispered into the ear of the dying person. It presents obstacles to be overcome, namely the fear that the tremendous figures, peaceful or wrathful, so easily induce in those not accustomed to their transcendent brilliance. It displays tempting sidetracks, the soft lights to the six lokas. And it limns the ultimate ends of the great pilgrimage: absorption into the bliss and power of the transcendent, life in heaven, or rebirth in this world.

Myths not only transmit information; they also inculcate attitudes toward it. How do we respond to a universe created in such-and-such a way, or to a destiny beyond the grave like this? We will see that afterlife myths suggest all sorts of responses: fear, wariness, gloom, wonder, ecstatic joy. Even more basically, they all are ways of articu-lating a fundamental human feeling: that our lives are somehow lived in a larger context than just birth to death in this particular world. We cannot normally remember our own conception or birth, nor can we truly imagine death, though we try. It seems something more must shape our lives, more than what we can know just in terms of the perspective of this world. The larger framework gives us hints, at least, about where we came from, where we are going, and what it's all about.

The distinguished poet William Butler Yeats once wrote, 'I have often had the fancy that there is some one myth for every man, which, if we but knew it, would make us understand all he did and thought.'[3] Many of us, if we were honest, would acknowledge a certain story, or at least image, we keep telling or describing to ourselves in some private chamber of consciousness. Though we share it with no one else, if broadcast it could tell the world much that is important about us.

At the same time, we cannot help but feel very important issues are left unresolved by one lifetime in one world: the vindication of right and wrong, empty places in hearts left by the loss of loved ones, all the unanswered questions.

Myths of the afterlife endeavor to fill in those blanks. It must be acknowledged that myths cannot deal fully with all doubts. Every myth opens with certain structures of the universe already set: one can always ask for a backstory telling how it happened to be that kind of cosmos in the first place. Those queries can go back and back, like the question children often ask: 'If God created the world, then who created God?'

No myth can explain everything. Perhaps that explains why so many different myths of the afterlife can be found, giving such different and often inconsistent information, calling up so many diverse 'feeling-tone' responses. Profound tensions between possible visions at odds with each other obtain in the world of afterlife mythology, and these tensions will be basic to the approach of this book.

We will now list a number of tensions or polarities in myths and concepts of the afterlife. Our approach in this study will be to present and discuss examples from various side of these dichotomies in each chapter. It will become clear that every major religion or religious culture is represented, if not in every corner, at least in a remarkable diversity of places. However, it will not be possible to present an example of every side for each faith. In each, one outlook will probably be dominant, the others present as minority opinions or recessive traits that may nonetheless supplant the dominant view given the right circumstances. Here are our areas of tension:

Tensions in Afterlife Myths and Doctrines

(1) *Taking afterlife seriously vs. virtual disbelief or unconcern about it*. Many rich mythologies depict a spectacular afterlife and an arduous pilgrimage-journey to fulfil it: Celtic, Egyptian, Native American, the Australian Dreamtime. On the other hand, the ancient Israelites, at least as represented in the Hebrew scriptures (Christian Old Testament), generally gave afterlife little mention, regarding God's rewards and punishments to be in this world.

(2) *Gloomy view of the afterlife vs. a bright, happy picture*. The ancient Mesopotamians, Japanese, and Greeks of the Homeric era affirmed the afterlife, but portrayed it as bare existence in a dismal underworld; for others it is, like the Buddhist western paradise, a place of sunny, splendid beauty and joy.

(3) *Where is the place of a deceased spirit?* Is it at the hearth or grave, or in an another world, such as heaven? In fact, we will find that some societies have postulated multiple souls so that aspects of the person can dwell in two or even three or more places.

(4) *Earthly immortality, such as that of the Taoist immortals, vs. immortality in another realm*. In some societies, it is said to be possible to attain a preternaturally long life, even virtual immortality, in this world, in this body, through the practice of esoteric forms of yoga, alchemy, or meditation, and that earthy longevity in effect takes the place of an eternal spiritual life in heaven.

(5) *Reincarnation on this earth vs. eternal life in a heavenly world.* Views of the afterlife in world religions break down fundamentally over whether reincarnation is affirmed, or the next life is always elsewhere then in this world. On the other hand, both options may be experienced, as in *The Tibetan Book of the Dead.* What about the resurrection of the body and a new heaven and earth? This belief is part of the picture too.

(6) *Is the afterlife theocentric or anthropocentric?* That is, does it emphasize only worship of God or mystical union, or does the ideal fulfilment of human concerns also have a place – even a central place – in heaven? These would be the likes of reunion on the other side with lovers and relatives, the enjoyment of innocent delights comparable to those of earth, such as dancing amid paradisal landscapes, or walking down the streets of golden cities. Does heaven include sublime sensuous and 'natural' loveliness, the beauty of birds, gardens, and music, or is it only 'spiritual'?

(7) *Is the afterlife static or progressive?* Is there spiritual education and progress in heaven, or are souls, once glory is attained, considered perfect, and hence incapable of further change?

(8) *Fear of ancestral or other spirits vs. respect and honor.* The fear of 'ghosts' is virtually a universal human dread; yet so also is the desire to reverence, even worship, the departed.

(9) *Community and religious solidarity vs. individual reward and punishment.* In some early societies, afterlife fate was often not highly differentiated among individuals, but was collective. Deceased children would be reborn in the same family; most persons from the same tribe would take essentially the same journey to the other world, save perhaps for exceptional rulers, shamans, or heroes. On the other hand, then and much later, rites and initiations, basically reflecting the common beliefs of a community and the power of its collective priests and prayers, could greatly assist in the transition of an individual, so that she or he was not solely dependent on personal virtue.

By way of contrast, some societies and religions have also emphasized strict individual moral judgment, sometimes, as in ancient Egypt, at the same time priestly and magical aids (e.g., mummification) were also deployed, leaving no reassurance unsecured. In Christianity too, judgment based on one's individual faith and moral life is emphasized, yet prayers and masses are also often said on behalf of the deceased, thus likewise employing the spiritual energy of the religious community to assist the individual's transition.

(10) *The difficult vs. the easy path.* In some traditions, adequate preparation for the afterlife requires not only strict morality, but also arduous regimens of yoga, initiations, and pilgrimage which change an individual into another, more adamant being, capable of deathlessness. In others, the secret is in its very simplicity, which emphasizes the overwhelming grace of God: simple faith in Christ or Amida, unfeigned devotion as in Hindu bhakti.

(11) *A personal and/or eschatological, linear view of history vs. cyclical time.* The western monotheistic religions, together with popular eastern views of reincarnation, indicate that both history and personal time are moving toward future goals, distant as they may be. But cyclical models, like that of primal societies that see life rotating between this world and the Dreamtime, or the Platonic and Hindu four declining ages, suggest one's place in the scheme is also conditioned by one's place in the cycle, and the afterlife itself may involve cycling between worlds. The paradox also leads to the issue of individual reward and punishment immediately after death vs. Last Day judgment. This tension, which particularly exists in the western monotheistic religions, Judaism, Christianity, and Islam, is a result of the Axial Age (to be discussed below), and its desire to find meaning in history. Summing-up and judgment at the end of days jostles with continuing belief in one's far more imminent individual journey and after-death judgment.[4]

(12) *Ordinary vs. extraordinary destinies after death.* Often, ordinary persons may have one kind of afterlife, warriors or heroes another. Most ancient Greeks went to the shadowy realm of Hades, but in time heroes could find rest in the Hesperides or the Isles of the Blest; ordinary Germanic people found themselves in the gloom of Hel, while warriors enjoyed warfare and feasting in the splendor of Valhalla. In medieval Christianity, saints went directly to heaven, while ordinary souls might need to undergo lengthy purification in Purgatory.

(13) *The One vs. the many.* Ultimately, the goal of the afterlife may not be reincarnation or life in another world, but union with Absolute, Unconditioned Reality: God, Brahman, Nirvana, the Clear Light of the Void. Separate existence falls away. In monotheistic religions, the experience of mystical union can make for tension with the need to maintain the distinction between Creator and creature.

Afterlife, Myth, and History

The distinguished analytic psychologist C. G. Jung once wrote:

When we look at human history, we see only what happens on the surface, and even this is distorted in the faded mirror of tradition. But what has really been happening eludes the inquiring eye of the historian, for the true historical event lies deeply buried, experienced by all and observed by none. It is the most private and subjective of psychic experiences. Wars, dynasties, social upheavals, conquests, and religions are but the superficial symptoms of a secret psychic attitude unknown even to the individual himself, and transmitted by no historian; perhaps the founders of religions give us the most information in this regard. The great events of world history are, at bottom, profoundly unimportant. In the last analysis, the essential thing is the life of the individual. This alone makes history, here alone do the the great transformations first take place, and the whole future, the whole history of the world, ultimately springs as a gigantic summation from these hidden sources in individuals. In our most private and most subjective lives we are not only the passive witnesses of our age, and its sufferers, but also its makers. We make our own epoch.[5]

Among the clues to psychological shifts which are the real, though deeply buried, makers of history, surely myth must rank as one of the most important. Jung held that dreams also gave clues to what was transpiring on the plane of group as well as individual unconscious, but then myths are the collective drams of the human race. By this of course one does not mean only schoolbook myths, or official myths, but those myths that are important to the 'individuals,' in their multitudes, of whom Jung writes.

One thinks not only of the important nineteenth-century recovery of national myths, such as the Finnish Kalevala or the Germanic Nibelungenlied, the Japanese Kojiki or the British cult of King Arthur and Camelot, at the roots of that century's nationalism, which in some cases had such bloody consequences in the next century. We recall also 'myths' told confidently and confidentially about what 'really' happened, perhaps on more parochial levels; whispered yarns of heroes and enemies modeling how 'we' in our little group think or act, told out-of-class in schoolyards or at office parties or in barracks or around campfires. Or one thinks of the way in which more recent 'myths' or urban legends about UFOs, or Satanists in day-care centers, or what 'they' don't want you to know, reflect the hopes and anxieties of numerous people, and they are heard so much that it seems they 'must be true.'

Myth and History: The Axial Age

A time there was in the past when the stories behind the current great religions were fresh and new, told with hope and dread from one ear to another. Of greatest significance of all are the changes in myth, views of human nature, views of the afterlife, and religious history that went with the 'Axial Age.'

The period around the fifth century B.C.E. was termed by the philosopher Karl Jaspers the Axial Turn, or Axial Age.[6] It was an important time of turning in many places on planet earth: the age of the great philosophers of India, China, and ancient Greece; and the time commencing the era of the founders of the great religions. Zoroaster, Confucius, Laozi (if historical), and the Buddha lived around then, as did the first makers of comparable changes in Hinduism (the earliest Upanishads) and Judaism (the Exile, Return, and codification of the Hebrew scriptures). The founders Jesus and Muhammad came half a millennium and a millennium later, but their work was in the same mold, and belongs to the Axial Age broadly understood.

Before, virtually all religion in the world had been in the archaic tribal or agricultural style, involving the polytheistic worship of local deities, even if adapted to the life of city-states like those of Greece, or agrarian empires like Egypt or Mesopotamia. But deep-level tensions were emerging: increasing travel and societal complexity made many people feel more individualized, less a part of a tribe or city. Above all, the 'discovery of history' meant the realization that we do not just live in seasonal cyclic time, always in the same place over against the mythic time of creation, but in linear, irreversible historical time in which things change and do not change back – and we get further and further from the mythic beginning.

This realization, undoubtedly a result of the invention of writing by which ongoing chronicles could be kept, profoundly affected religious consciousness. For being left stranded in linear time brought a sense of the 'terror of history,' as Mircea Eliade called it. In any case that gloomy perspective must have seemed natural to most ordinary ancient people, for to them history was all too often mostly a matter of plague, famine, and one conquering army after another marching across one's fields. History, they desperately hoped, must also have a larger meaning, or at least a way of escape from its toils. Now that the irreversible march of history had been seen for what it was, the explanation and way of egress could not be only a return – such as was symbolized in so many ancient New Year's rites – to an increasingly remote mythic time of origins. It had to look upward and forward as well, to an end when all tears would be wiped away, and the glory of which was so great as to cause even the sorrows of all time to fade away

That was the burden of hope brought by the great religious founders as they turned the Axial Age and set its aftermath rolling down the years. That these divine voices were born and bred *within* historical time was significant; they were not just mythic figures out of some equally mythic long ago. Jesus, in the words of the Christian creed, 'suffered under Pontius Pilate,' a quite historical figure, and yet of his birth the familiar Christmas carol, addressing Bethlehem, sings, 'The hopes and fears of all the years/are met in thee tonight.'

The founders and their religions offered, beyond somewhat sanctifying history by appearing in the midst of it, four messages for seeing, and experiencing, history as more than just one bad thing after another. These points are given different emphasis in the different faiths, one or two not appearing at all in some, and in other cases are not fully articulated until later in the religion's history. But overall they give a sense of what the Axial Age revolution meant to religion and to the afterlife; the great majority of humankind are now, at least culturally, within the orbit of a religion founded or significantly modified in response to that era. Here are four areas of Axial Age religious revolution:

(1) *Eschatology.* An End to history is coming, at a day of judgment when its mysterious meaning will be made clear, and justice will be administered to the actors in history: the Jewish, Christian, and Islamic Last Day, the Buddhist coming of the future Buddha Maitreya.

(2) *A definite method of salvation in an afterlife.* While the eschatological Last Day at the end of history is pretty much a development of the Axial Age with its discovery of history, as we know various concepts of the afterlife are much older. But the new teachers, claiming greater universality in their doctrine, presented a pattern of salvation through faith, morality, and rites applicable to all humankind. This schema was typically far more precise and individualized than what went before, putting as central for all *individual* faith, morality, and reception of rites. Hence came a new Axial Age religious emphasis on the individual. Karma was for in each individual person in the east, as was personal judgment at death in the west, even if the

individual reckoning at the hour of departure might have been in some tension with an End of Days eschatology and final judgment later.

(3) *Methods for mystical union with the One outside of time and history.* Yoga, attaining nirvana, the mystical traditions of all religions, usually fully developed a little after the Axial Age, are perhaps partly in reaction against its tension and change.

(4) *Rules of life and ways of organizing society that make even ordinary life in this world better.* Practical Axial Age religion legislates everyday life in an attempt to make it satisfyingly structured over against the chaos of history, even a kind of foretaste of coming paradise: the Jewish Halakah, Islamic Shari'a, Confucian code, Laws of Manu.

Along with these developments went an explosion of mythological, folkloric, and doctrinal interest in the afterlife. Although colorful accounts of the afterlife obtained in many primal societies and initiatory religions, along with others such as the Semitic and Homeric Greek in which it tended to be dank and dismal, now bright heavens were part of most major universal faiths. Early Christianity, for example, showed a clear distinction between heaven and hell, the afterlife abodes respectively of the saved and unsaved. The new faith also formed doctrines defining how the sacrifice of Christ is applied to individual believers, showing how each individual could be saved and brought into the realm of the righteous by a combination of right faith, good works, and sacramental grace received through baptism, holy communion, and forgiveness of sins.

Another characteristic of the Axial Age religions hardly less important than the forgoing was the production of a scripture believed to be uniquely inspired: the Bible, the Quran, the Confucian 'classics,' the Buddhist sutras. Surely this is a concomitant of the invention of writing along with the crisis of historical consciousness which made for the Axial Age in the first place. The new day of literacy and spiritual exactitude called for definite dicta, set down in writing, to anchor young faiths looking forward to world-spanning futures.

A text like this, birthed in the nascent religion, was able to spell out more carefully than before what was necessary for salvation. The process was therefore both individual and communal, since the sacred texts were studied in community, but the individual in this Axial Age faith was expected to take some personal responsibility for his or her after-death state. We will see how this necessity was expressed in myths and stories of the afterlife. It is well known what kind of impact on history these bibles of the world have had. One way or another, their visions of the afterlife, and what was needed to win heaven, have issued orders mobilizing the saints and soldiers who made history down through the long annals of those faiths.

Myth and History: The Sequel

Subsequent views of after-death states in the Axial Age religions, recounted in story, surely reflect over and over the hopes and anxieties of the living, thereby no less interfacing with history. Here for reasons of space we will give only examples from Christianity, but others will be advanced later. The Dialogues of the sixth century Pope Gregory the Great contain a Near-Death experience that lacks nothing to suggest both anxiety and the prospect of bliss on the other side. During a plague:

> A certain soldier in this city of ours happened to be struck down. He was drawn out of his body and lay lifeless, but he soon returned [to life] and described what befell him. At that time there were many people experiencing these things. He said that there was a bridge, under which ran a black, gloomy river which breathed forth an intolerably foul-smelling vapor. But across the bridge there were delightful meadows carpeted with green grass and sweet-smelling flowers. The meadows seemed to be meeting places for people clothed in white. Such a pleasant odor filled the air that the sweet smell by itself was enough to satisfy [the hunger of] the inhabitants who were strolling there . . .[7]

The pontiff goes on to relate how crossing that bridge was a test. An unjust person, endeavoring to cross, would slip and fall into the dark and stinking water beneath. An unworthy elder of an ecclesiastical family lay under the bridge in the odious slime, weighted down by a great iron chain, because 'when he was ordered to punish someone he used to inflict blows more out of a love of cruelty than out of obedience.' Another individual, a certain Stephan, slipped but then became an object of contest between angelic and demonic beings: hideous creatures came up from below, and grabbed him by the hips to pull him down; then 'very splendid men dressed in white' began to lift him back up by the arms. But while this human tug-of-war was going on, the observant soldier was called back to his body, so he never knew how the struggle came out.[8]

Later medieval visions, leading up to the great panorama of Dante's Divine Comedy, emphasized still more the usual geography of hell: the fires, pits, furnaces, and sadistic demons testing endlessly ingenious tortures on their eternal victims. The 1206 *Vision of Thurkill*, recounting the revelations given that English peasant, tells us that, in addition to those diabolical staples, he saw an arena with tiered seats, where devils sat delightedly watching one torture after another administered to the damned for their entertainment; still higher up, on a nearby mountain, the saints were observing the same spectacle, no doubt with satisfaction that divine justice was being vindicated.[9]

Medieval visions of heaven were no less rich and graphic. Mechthild of Magdeburg (c. 1207–1282), for example, saw three heavens. First was an earthly paradise of wondrous gardens, sweet-smelling air, and gentle rivers, where she met such Old Testament worthies as Enoch and Elijah. Then she entered a second heaven like an immense domed celestial cathedral with ten levels or 'choirs' of Christian angels and saints where, interestingly, holy women occupied the tenth and highest level, above even the apostles on the ninth. A third heaven towered still higher; there God dwelt in his palace, and Christ's bridal chamber was likewise found. Alone among the saints, the virginal holy women of the tenth rank were allowed to enter this bridal chamber, where Christ himself may favor them with an embrace and a kiss from his sacred lips.[10]

How do such visions as these help us interpret medieval history? One may sometimes wonder why, if medievals believed as strongly as it seems in such graphic postmortem rewards and punishments, their rapacious behavior so often appears to make a quite different statement? Aldous Huxley put it this way: 'A firm conviction of the material reality of Hell never prevented medieval Christians from doing what their ambition, lust or covetousness suggested.'[11]

The same author added it is no less the case with us moderns. Even if a sense of hell has, for some, faded, many insist on drinking alcohol or smoking tobacco despite the quite this-worldly evidence presented in the millions ravaged by alcoholism or lung cancer. But what comes through accounts like Thurkill's, Gregory's, or Mechtild's is not only the specifics of hell, but no less a pervasive sense of anxiety; one is never quite sure whether one will cross the bridge without slipping, or win the bridal chamber of the divine lover. It is out of anxiety, more than defiance of a sure thing, that stems the wariness which so easily explodes in violence, or gluttony on the occasion when the platter is full, even as the need to control anxiety undoubtedly explains much problem drinking and smoking today despite highly visible dismal results.

Medieval anxiety and wariness came from many sources: abundance or famine, health or plague, war or peace, love or neglect within families were always uncertain possibilities here and now; add to this the tensions of celibacy for the regiments of medieval religious, many of whom were among the afterlife visionaries. Perhaps it was not only nervous apprehension about the afterlife that prompted such visions, but just as much gnawing anxiety about this life. A worried world and a worrisome afterlife interpret each other, and the incipient 'myths' of the long journey help turn the wheels of Jung's 'hidden sources' within individuals that ultimately roll the large-scale history of the world down the highways of time.

By way of contrast, we might briefly advance centuries ahead to the afterlife of late Victorian England and America. Take the bestselling novels of Elizabeth Stuart Phelps, especially *The Gates Ajar* (1868) and *Beyond the Gates* (1883), which vividly portray heaven as a place of happy families united forever, abiding in lovely homes, without hint of tears or trouble. (There is little mention of hell.) The first book is based on conversation among women who endeavor to deal with the loss of loved ones in the recently concluded Civil War, thinking out of their own insight and in some defiance of the Calvinist orthodoxy of their New England background. The second novel, *Beyond the Gates*, relates the fictional visions of a woman of about forty, who is desperately ill, indeed near death.[12] Guided by her predeceased father, she visited a heaven of gorgeous scenery, cozy and comfortable homes, reunion with a one-time earthly lover, and the opportunity to hear a symphony conducted by none other than Beethoven himself, or to hear a sermon from the lips of St. John the Apostle.

It is clear that these stories epitomize the Victorian idealization of the family, aspirations to 'high' culture, and no less the era's preoccupation with death. The rising romantic view of love extended, in popular culture, to an exalted view of the family which presumably followed marriage as the proper culmination of such love, and then – given the sad fact that most nineteenth-century families experienced the deaths of children, and all too often of young husbands and wives as well – to the elaborate mourning customs, black crepe and all, that distinguish the period. At the same time, popular religion also witnessed, in some quarters, the slow recession of Satan, hell, and forensic postmortem judgment, influenced as it was by Swedenborgianism,

Spiritualism, and the Enlightenment's and romanticism's relatively benign views of God.

But do the new anthropocentric Victorian views of the afterlife really interact with world history as a whole? We will return to this issue. For now, it may be sufficient to suggest the background of Elizabeth Phelps' vision in the terrible bloodbath of the American Civil War, that she was a pioneer feminist (her heavens are inevitably seen through women's eyes), and to mention also the social movements of the coming 'progressive era,' the 1890s and early 1900s: temperance, women's right to vote, labor reform (including reform of the evil of child labor), improved education, and world peace (as brutally as that hope was affronted in 1914). All these causes could be seen as profoundly interacting with visions of the archetypal happy family, whether on this or on the other side of life.

Is Myth True?

Are the stories of the lives of the Axial Age founders and saviors, as well as those of countless other saints and reformers with some claim to historicity, to be taken as myths? It has been said that Christianity, for example, is not myth because of its historicity, indeed the central place it gives to God acting in history. Perhaps so, if one takes the common definition of a myth as a story that is not true, or a story only set in a mythic time before history. Our approach, however, has been to see myth as a narrative which sets down in story form a society's basic structures and organization, values and proper modes of behavior, and finally the meaning of human life in the largest possible context, the universe itself – and to emphasize that a society's views of the afterlife can deeply reflect the innermost values of that society and its individual constituents.

Whether a given story, or story-figure, is historical, quasi-historical, or entirely fictional should not make too much difference to such understanding, so long as it plays the value-bearing role. In fact, not only is the whole idea of history as we know it relatively late – arriving with writing and the Axial Age – but historical consciousness barely affected the religious minds of good numbers of humans, largely peasants, until well into the twentieth century in some places. One wonders if, around 1950, the way a non-literate Hindu peasant envisioned Krishna, or a Latin American Catholic peasant envisioned Christ, was really much different, even though from the scholar's point of view one might be thought more historical than the other. But to both worshipers 'on the ground,' the spiritual being was a luminous, miracle-working man with power to answer prayer and bring into heaven. Both are mythic in our sense, offering a link to our ultimate environment and meaning in visual, even tangible, form.

Thus the word myth is used here in a positive sense, without any implication of judgment as to whether the story is true or false. One could hold to the theology concerning Christ of the most conservative churches and still recognize that the Christian story, though literally true, nonetheless functions exactly like any myth within the communities in which it is held to convey all-powerful meaning. Indeed, many of the church fathers did in effect take this position, as they compared Christ to such mythic figures as Hercules, the dying-rising gods of the Mysteries such as Orpheus, or Sol Invictus, the invincible sun of the late Roman Empire; Eusebius of Caesarea in his *Praeparatio Evangelica* presents these comparisons in a way that only enhanced the final significance of the Nazarene.

Are Afterlife Beliefs True?

Finally, what about the veridicality of afterlife beliefs? Can life after death be proved? It is not the purpose of this book to answer that eternal question, but a few remarks may be in order.

Probably no issue better illustrates how an answer can be built into the methodology meant to investigate a question. One methodology for seeking out the truth about the afterlife is dependence on religious authority, scriptural and traditional. Obviously, from a rational point of view, this authority is no better than that which can be ascribed the source. But the method does have a larger significance than that sort of rationalistic reductionism, for points to the fact that religion, and therefore religious beliefs such as those about death and afterlife, is always social. Beliefs are therefore not just truth-conveying, they are also social bonds.

Anyone who has been to a traditionally religious funeral, or to a congregational service in which salvation after death is proclaimed, is aware that afterlife beliefs not only look beyond this life. They also bring together families and communities in this life, especially at times when catharsis and re-bonding the family and community are important. Religion is communal. No ordinary religion would be in the least convincing if it were held by only one person; when it is held by two or more, it becomes healing and, in a real sense, convincing, since we, most of us, seem to need to share whatever conceptions we have of life, death, and beyond as we let them complete our humanity. This does not mean such beliefs are bad, even if otherwise unverifiable; it only affirms that we humans *are* social creatures, that beliefs can have a healing social role, and their real if unacknowledged validity may in large part lie in this role.

Second, what about alleged empirical methods for seeking out the facts about the afterlife? Here too, an answer is built into the method. Since that method generally assumes only that which is observable by scientific means to be reliable, it is likely to come up with a negative answer, reporting back that nothing verifiable by science's quantifiable or physical means of repeatable observation or experiment can be found to validate after-death survival.

To be sure, results can be found in the records of scientific psychical research, including the study of near-death experiences, which challenge that conclusion. But mainstream scientists generally discount those claims, often no doubt because they are simply not repeatable under identical conditions, or compatible with the assumptions about nature that underlie empirical research in the first place. There are hints of developments on the cutting edges of quantum and complexity theory that may offer other theoretical frameworks; here we await further developments.

Finally, there is what might be called the experiential or mystical basis for afterlife beliefs. Few can remember their own coming into consciousness in the womb, or can truly imagine their own death as the absolute cutting-off of consciousness. At the same time, states of consciousness are claimed in which the timelessness and deathlessness of the experiencer was beyond doubt. How much this proves depends, of course, on how much one thinks that the self can truly know its own nature, quite apart from rational analysis of a sort imposed by the pervasive scientific culture of external empiricism within which we live, and which has been right about enough pertaining to nature to fabricate marvelous technological support-systems for human life. But does this mean it knows all about life and death?

In any case, it is subjective experience which moves closest to the realm of myth, for myth does suggest one can move in story and vision beyond the circles of this world, and myth can evoke a sense of wonder not dissimilar to the timeless state. In this study, however, we will generally set aside these final questions, and stay with the stories.

It remains only to reiterate that after-death beliefs and the culture, semi-secular as well as religious, in which they dwell are in profound interaction. One can learn much about a culture, whether it be early medieval anxiety or Victorian idealization of family life, from how it builds its other world, and likewise that invisible empyrean will construct its cathedrals as surely as bricks and mortar. Let us now turn to the exciting tale of those heavenly exchanges.

Chapter 2

Hungry and Happy Fields of the Dead: Gloomy vs. Bright Views of the Afterlife

Shy Voices from the Land of Silence

Our early ancestors before the Axial Age did not always enjoy a cheerful picture of the afterlife. Life was hard for most of the living, and the shadow-life of the dead seemed correspondingly dismal and tenuous, at first even for heroes. In a famous scene in Homer's Odyssey, Odysseus goes to the underworld in order to consult the soul of Teiresias, a great seer, as to what he must do in order to return home.

Odysseus was informed that first he had to sacrifice two sheep, for the departed are mere 'empty shells' flitting mindlessly about till they take a sip of blood. A bit of that fluid of life will restore them long enough to speak to a mortal visitor. By this sanguinary means Odysseus conversed not only with Teiresias, but also with such former comrades in the Trojan War as Achilles and Agamemnon (whom he learns was murdered by his wife on his return home), and with his own mother. One can well understand Odysseus' eagerness to depart Persephone's dark and ghostly realm; of it Achilles goes so far as to say that he would rather be a poor man's ploughman in the land of the living than king over all the dead.[13]

Moving to the ancient Semitic world, we find that generally the Hebrew scriptures (the Christian Old Testament) offer very little on an afterlife, apart from a few ambiguous passages. God's rewards and punishments are met with in this life. The deceased at best are consigned to a shadowy Sheol, rather like Homer's underworld. The Psalmist who plaintively queried, 'O Lord, how long shall the wicked, how long shall the wicked exult?' (Ps. 94:3) could then only trust that

'Blessed is the man whom thou dost chasten, O Lord' (94:12); 'If the Lord had not been my help, my soul would soon have dwelt in the land of silence' (94:17). 'For in death there is no remembrance of thee; in Sheol who can give thee praise?' (Ps. 6: 5).

Most memorable is the incident when King Saul, desperate as the Philistines advanced against him in great strength, insisted his servants bring to him a witch or medium from Endor, to call up the spirit of the great prophet Samuel. The latter rose up out of the earth, in appearance an old man wrapped in a robe, who irritably asked the hapless Saul why he had disturbed him. When the harried monarch tried to explain, the prophet could only tell him – as he had in life – that the Lord had turned against him for his disobedience. Soon enough Samuel's harsh strictures were vindicated. Saul was decisively defeated, severely wounded, and then died by falling on his own sword (I Sam. 28: 6–25, 31:5). A scattering of more positive views of the afterlife begin to appear in very late Hebrew literature, probably influenced by Zoroastrian sources.

The ancient Israelites' Semitic kinsmen, the Babylonians and Canaanites, held to a similarly bleak picture of the afterlife. Their dead, confined to a dim underworld realm, require memorial offerings to restrain them from harming the living. *The Epic of Gilgamesh*, the most famous example of Sumerian and Babylonian literature, and perhaps the oldest extant written story in the world, relates that hero's attempt to obtain immortality in this life rather than abide in the 'house of dust.' He sought help from Utnapishtim, the Babylonian Noah who, surviving the Flood, uniquely attained deathlessness for himself and his wife. That worthy eventually told Gilgamesh of a plant able to renew youth. Through great effort, the hero found and plucked the medicine of immortality. But on his way home, the lucky mortal took time out to bathe in a pool, carelessly leaving the precious plant on the ground, where an unlikely creature took it and gained the power of rejuvenation instead.

Stephen Mitchell, in the Introduction to his translation of Gilgamesh, comments that the hero's heedless act seems comparable to other last-minute mistakes in myths and folktales, like Orpheus' absent-minded glance at Eurydice on the way out of Hades. 'There is always something fated about these mistakes,' Mitchell adds; 'they don't seem like accidents . . . we feel they had to happen.'[14] In a semi-comic African tale, a toad thought he should carry the elixir of immortality to humankind instead of the snake, and of course spilled it on the second hop; only the serpent, having already tested the fabulous potion, remained able to shed his skin and renew his life indefinitely. In Gilgamesh, as in Africa and in the Garden of Eden story, the spoiler is a snake. Here, though, the snake is innocent; he just saw the forgotten plant and thought it looked good to eat. A few lines say it all:

> A snake smelled its fragrance, stealthily
> it crawled up and carried the plant away.
> As it disappeared, it cast off its skin.[15]

Sorrowfully, Gilgamesh realized that immortality is reserved for divine beings alone, and accepted the hard truth that mortals must die.

Traveling further east, we come to the Chinese underworld called the Yellow Springs and the Japanese equivalent, Yomi, where according to some Shinto mythology the dead can only decay, and whose exits are guarded by horrible female monsters. Once one has eaten of the food of Yomi, it is impossible to return to the above-ground land of the living. The primal parents of humanity, Izanagi and Izanami, learned this the hard way.

After an orgy of procreation in which innumerable gods and lands were made, Izanami, the first mother, died giving birth to the fire-god. She descended to Yomi. Her spouse, Izanagi, after wailing bitterly, made his way down the 'eighty road-windings' of the dark path toward the empire of the dead to rescue her. Alas, she had already partaken of its food, and like Persephone in the comparable Greek myth of Hades, was condemned to stay. Unlike the daughter of Demeter, the Japanese goddess would not even have short respites above, though she was now empress below.

But Izanami remonstrated with her spouse for his tardiness in coming for her. Izanagi, now full of anger as well as sorrow, retreated, pursued by hags till he came once more into the sun. He and his former consort exchanged taunts: Izanagi said he would divorce her; she screamed in retaliation that if he did she would bring a thousand souls daily into her dismal realm. He replied if she did that, he would give life to 1,500 with every new day. Thus, despite death, life would prevail in the outer world.[16] But so far as the dead were concerned, their ghostly ongoing existence offered little but darkness and perhaps bad dreams.

The Coming of Hope

Toward the end of the pre-Axial Age period, glimmers of light regarding a brighter afterlife began to appear in inscriptions, mythic literature, and mystery cults like those of Orpheus or Isis. At first the sparsely populated paradises were reserved for kings, heroes, or initiates, but gradually became more and more open, until finally all those who are good, or properly prepared ritually, could gain admission. (Of course it may be the case that non-literate popular religion long held robust images of life after death on the part of commoners as well as elites, but most of this has been lost, except as reflected in folklore collected much later.)

So it is that ancient Egyptians are well known for their interest in postmortem states, though at first, so far as we know from inscriptions, they regarded immortality reserved for the pharaoh, who was Horus during life and resuscitated as Osiris after death. According to the very early Pyramid Texts, the ruler's spirit joined the sun god Ra in his solar ship to sail with him through daylight skies, and pass through the dark underworld at night. Later the afterlife was opened first to priests and officials, and finally to all Pharaoh's subjects. The just lived in a community centered around Osiris, while the unrighteous suffered in a dark, chaotic realm.

The deceased first had to pass through a number of hazards on the underworld journey. These mainly consisted of fending off demons. That task required knowing the demons' secret names, plus certain magical spells. For example, to circumvent demons and advance along the grueling journey, it was advisable to use spells that would turn one into a hawk, goose, swallow, serpent, crocodile, and phoenix: 'I fly like a hawk, I cackle like a goose . . . I advance to the realm of the stargods. The realms of Ma'at are open to me . . . I rise up like Ra . . . my heart, once brought low, is made strong. I am a spirit in heaven, and mighty upon earth!'[17]

All this information was helpfully supplied in funerary texts, together with guiding maps of the underworld. Finally the pilgrim arrived at the throne of Osiris himself, where his soul was weighed against a feather; those who successfully passed this test entered into their reward, while all others were doomed to darkness.

But it must be noted the decision was not entirely on moral grounds, since to get to that throne of judgment the mortal traveler first had to follow the charts and contend with demons. It also helped if the physical body was preserved, hence mummification. Once past the gates, the deceased could enjoy the life of the gods, which sounds like nothing more nor less than the good life here on earth: an endless round of partying and lovemaking in a land similar to Egypt, with a broad river running down its center. In more exalted afterlife images, the soul was united with Osiris, eternal lord of life.[18]

Islands of the Blest

Greek mythology offered, along with the dark realm of Hades, the alternative of the Isles of the Blest, called the Elysian Fields or Elysium in Homer's Odyssey, where it is the destination of Menelaus, husband of Helen, or the Hesperides, after Hesperos, the Evening Star. The Hesperides were the location of the 'rich, golden apples on the tree bearing fruit beyond glorious Ocean,'[19] which Heracles took after slaying Ladon, the dragon who guarded them. In either case the sacred site is located in the far west, probably beyond the Pillars of Hercules (Straits of Gibraltar) in the western ocean; it is natural to locate the place of departed souls toward the sunset. Entry to these Enchanted Islands was reserved to a privileged few; the happy dead were the greatest of all heroes from the mythic age and the Trojan War.

The lore of many nations is full of fascinating enchanted lands at or beyond the frontiers of the known world, usually far beyond the horizons of the great sea, whether Elysium or the Celtic Avalon or Plato's Atlantis to the west, or the Uttermost West, the Undying Lands of Aman, to which elves and heroes pass from the Grey Havens in the modern mythology of J. R. R. Tolkien's *The Lord of the Rings*. To the sunrise East equivalents are Shambhala, the Garden of Eden, or the Sino-Japanese island of immortals, Penglai or Horai.

Often these fabulous sites have overtones of being lands of the dead, or places of auspicious rebirth. Many scholars surmise the Celtic Other World was originally such a place, but after Christianization and knowledge of the new faith's heaven and hell, the overseas or underground paradises became fairylands instead. In cosmic religion these lands of magic and of the dead often reflect what is called horizontal cosmology, being on the same plane as our world but over many waters or beyond distant mountain ranges; the alternative is the vertical cosmology of heaven above and underworld beneath, perhaps as levels on a cosmic tree or mountain like that of the ancient Norse or

Hindus. In old Norse religion, Hel, the destination of ordinary folk not eligible to join the noble Aesir warriors in Valhalla, was apparently underground; accounts also report that the dead entered a realm under the mountains, where occasionally the sound of their feasting and merriment could be heard by outsiders. The Saami or Lapps believed that their shamans might fly into mountains in trance to retrieve lost souls or communicate with the dead.[20] But Axial Age or historical religions almost inevitably came to think in terms of vertical cosmology, when they did not think of after-death states as outside our space and time entirely.

Returning to the ancient world, what have been called mystery religions offered the prospect of a happy afterlife to a broader range of persons than heroes alone, if they were willing to undertake the ordeal of initiation. Rites such as those of Eleusis, Isis, Bacchus, or Mithras promised their initiates immortal life with their deity. The last, Mithras, a heroic divine figure of Persian background, represented the unconquerable sun; he had created the world by an act of slaying a bull, reproduced in statues throughout the Mithraic world. The bull was perhaps a symbol of primordial chaos, but even more he betokened death and transformation; his horns represented the moon, eternal symbol of dark death followed by bright renewal, while his blood and semen were life-giving.

The worship of Mithras, popular particularly with Roman military men, may have involved baptism of initiates with the blood of a sacrificial bull, and festive banquets in the god's honor.[21] The mithraeum, or Mithraic place of worship, found throughout the Roman world from Britain to the Near East, contained elaborate astrological symbolism believed by some scholars to represent the descent of the soul and its return through various planetary levels to the eternal realm of the stars.

Reinforcement: The Afterlife in the Axial Age Religions

With the advent of the Axial Age, three points can be noted about views of the afterlife, in supplement to the general features of Axial Age religion already presented, such as the sanctification of scripture, increased individualization of faith and salvation, and end-of-linear-history eschatology. These are tendencies, not absolutes, often merely continuing and intensifying movements already in place. Yet the Axial

Age religions magnified them sufficiently to change contours of religious life from then on. Here they are:

(1) In Axial Age religion, the afterlife becomes more vivid and more precisely defined, often with the aid of the just-mentioned authoritative written scriptures and traditions that were inevitably part of its equipment. (Remember, the Axial Age religion were no doubt an indirect result of that monumental advance, the invention of writing, and made full use of its advantages over oral and shamanic transmission of doctrine.)

(2) The states of the afterlife become more polarized, and more closely tied to moral as well as ritual preparation. Despite the possibility of intermediate states, the Axial Age religions tended to emphasize stark individual choice between heaven and hell, or good and bad reincarnations.

(3) The afterlife was thus more individualized, based in individual faith or merit. It was accessible to everyone, and at the same time more closely keyed to one's individual choices. As we have seen, in cosmic religion afterlife, most ordinary people shared about the same destiny, usual dismal, with only great heroes or pharaohs enjoying something better. Or else, as in many tribal cultures, most people took the same trail or the same ship to the other world – often a mirror image of ours – without great distinction, though shamans might go ahead as guides. Now, each individual however humble can expect to be sternly judged and sent to precisely the correct fate according to his deservings.

Zoroastrianism: Light against the Lie

Let us see how this worked out in practice. We might begin with Zoroastrianism, perhaps the first and in many ways the prototype of the Axial Age religion, for it may well have profoundly influenced Judaism, Christianity, Islam, and even Buddhism in regard to key religious factors that are distinctive of the Axial Age.

Like all the Axial Age faiths (except later Hinduism, which however passed through sometimes comparable stages of development), Zoroastrianism is the work of a founder in historical time, with whose life and message it deeply identifies, seeing him as a turning point (axle) in history. As with the others also, his life is enshrouded with myth, legend, and controversy, so much so that even his existence has been debated. Yet, no less than with the other founders, the traditional story of his life vitally important for understanding what he has meant as a religious figure.

The Persian people of his time were cousins of the Indo-European or Aryan people of ancient Vedic India – the alternative name of the country, Iran, is a variant of Aryan. They were served by priests called *zaotar* or *hotar* like the brahmins of India, and their religion likewise centered around a sacred fire, the sacrifice of cattle, and a sacred drink, *haoma*, comparable to the soma – perhaps hallucinogenic – of the Vedas. With all this Zarathustra, though a priest himself, was profoundly dissatisfied, and he suffered the consequences of his doubt; it is said he was shunned and cast out by kin and community.

Even the dates of Zarathustra (Zoroaster to the Greeks) have been given wildly varying values. Those most widely accepted today seem to be 628–551 B.C.E., which would put him appropriately right before Jasper's Axial Age, after the invention of writing, and at a time when history was visibly and irreversibly being made as Persia was united under Cyrus I and other rulers, ultimately to be made into the vast Persian Empire of Cyrus the Great, who ascended the throne in 559, eight years before Zarathustra's putative death.[22] Certainly enough was going on in this prophet's lifetime to suggest dramatically changing times full of the hope and terror of history, calling for a new kind of religious vision.

The traditional story has it that this vision came quite literally. Zoroaster became a wanderer, and his questioning mind remained restless. In the Gathas, poems ascribed to him, he repeatedly intercedes passionately on behalf *gaush uva*, the soul of the cow, who represents the downtrodden and oppressed, humans as well as animals, and decried the ritual sacrifice of harmless beasts in such lines as:

> Mazda has foretold
> the evil they will suffer
> when they destroy the life of the cow
> with exultant shrieks.
> The Worshipers of Falsehood prefer
> the power of the illicitly wealthy karapans
> instead of the Truth.[23]

Moreover, Zarathustra considered *haoma* to be the instrument of the priests he contemptuously called *karapans*, murmurers and moaners, and held the only fire he needed was the light of Ahura Mazda, the high god himself. In all, he yearned for a religion dealing with larger issues than ritual, focused on ethics and direct prayer to the supreme deity, a faith in which the opposition between *asha*, 'truth,' and *druj*, 'the lie,' traditional themes in Iranian belief, was central.

One day, by a stream where he was gathering water for ablutions, Zarathustra was met by a figure in shining white, who took him away, perhaps to heaven itself, for an encounter with six holy figures, including Ahura Mazda, Lord of Light. Before, in pre-Zoroastrian religion, Mazda was, with Mithra (the sun-deity who became the deity of the Greco-Roman cult) and Apam Napat, guardian of honesty and oath-keeping, three great Ahura or Lords. But in Zarathustra's visions Mazda became the one supreme monotheistic God, the others joining the ranks of archangelic figures who served the cause of Truth in the ceaseless battle against the Lie.

The Zoroastrian worldview, painting that conflict on a large canvass, declared that the universe was the scene of war to the death between good and evil. The hosts of Ahura Mazda, Lord of Light, are ranged against his eternal foe, Angra Mainyu, Lord of the Lie, and his demons of darkness. In this struggle, human beings are used by Ahura Mazda as a kind of bait, for the evil one tries to turn them to his side through seductive temptations. But when we resist, remaining loyal to the good, the dark power is weakened by so much, and Ahura Mazda gains.

How are these personal triumphs rewarded in terms of individual afterlife? Zoroastrianism teaches that after a three-day waiting period, the soul of the deceased is taken into the presence of mighty angelic judges of the dead, who weigh the soul. If good tips the balance, the entrant into the afterlife perceives a beautiful maiden, representing a clear conscience. But if judgment goes the other way, he beholds the ugly face of a twisted mind instead.

After this decision, all spirits proceed across the Chinvat Bridge, which swings above the abyss of hell as it leads to heaven. For the righteous, that span is a broad highway into the House of Song, as the blessed realm is called. But for those who served Angra Mainyu, the way turns narrow as a razor; losing balance, their hapless souls slip down into the dismal underworld below. The good news is that, at the end of the warlike world-drama, Ahura Mazda will empty both heaven and hell; the wicked will be purged of their sin; and all will live together in a paradisal new earth.

For the ultimate outcome is not in doubt. At the appointed time a savior, Saoshyant, will appear to work the final vanquishing of evil, restoring creation to its original perfection. Hell will be closed, its inhabitants purified and enabled to join the righteous, and the demonic armies destroyed. All humanity will be given a wonderful drink of immortality, as the world becomes as endlessly beautiful and benign as its maker, the Lord of Light, had intended at the outset. But now goodness is everlasting; the invasion by the Lie and the great war will not be repeated.[24]

In this irreversible eschatological process we see plain the Axial Age outlook: it is clear that Ahura Mazda, sovereign over history, will win the war in the end; his will be a once-for-all victory, and time even now moves one-way toward that consummation. The individual's fate is also particularized, with personal judgment, and confrontation with one's own conscience. Even if these two ends, individual judgment at the end of individual life and universal judgment at the end of history, do not entirely fit comfortably together, both must be maintained to uphold both the historicism and enhanced individualism of the Axial Age. (This conundrum is no less apparent in other Axial faiths, such as Judaism, Christianity, Islam, Buddhism, and Hinduism, which in various ways try to correlate the two through such means as hour-of-death plus last-day judgments of each person. One finds mediating intermediate states such as Purgatory or, in Islam, al-Barzakh; further East, there is the coexistence of individual karma and world-cycles.)

Questions that Changed the World

The movement from Cosmic to Axial Age beliefs about the personal afterlife is well expressed in a Hindu context in the Katha Upanishad. This text, generally considered to be from the Axial period, the fifth or sixth century B.C.E., reveals splendidly the intrusion of new kinds of thoughts like those that disturbed Zarathustra. The Katha begins with the account of a young man named Nachiketa. Nachiketa's crusty old brahmin father presented a sacrifice of the Vedic sort in which he was supposed to offer all his possessions, but was careful to present only old and scroungy cattle. The boy, shocked by this stinginess, told his father he also was one of his possessions: to whom he would give his son? The irritated parent responded that he would give him to Yama, the ancient King of the Dead.

The noble Nachiketa, believing his father's word must be kept, did so even at what he thought at the time would be at the cost of his own life, for generally Death keeps what he receives, until life's time comes round again in accordance with the timeless cycles. 'Like corn, a man ripens and falls to the ground; like corn, he springs up again in his season,' spoke Nachiketa in consolation to his father.[25] But then something interesting happened. Arriving at the palace of Death, the young brahmin found the dark king not at home, and was forced to wait, a violation of ancient codes of hospitality that even as sovereign a prince as Yama was obliged to honor. When Yama returned, and his courtiers informed their master that, 'A Brahmin, like to a flame of fire, entered thy house as a guest, and thou wast not there,' in compensation the Lord of Death offered the sincere young intruder three boons.[26]

The initial two wishes were clearly rooted in the traditional Cosmic and Vedic world, with its cycles, its relationships, its deities empowered in and through nature, not above or apart from it. Nachiketa first asked that his father's anger be appeased; this wish concerned the worldly social obligations of patriarchal society.

Second, he asked to know the fire sacrifice that led to heaven, for the power of sacrifice extends from this world to the next. But that too was only a worldly matter, too, for life in the Vedic heavens extended only as long as the cosmic energy generated by the rite held out. Depending on one's skill and power, it might assure bliss for a very long time, but being just a matter of technical craft, it would ultimately wear down, for within the cosmos there is no such thing as perpetual motion or energy. With the questions of his guest so far, Yama was well pleased.

But the third question was a shift to another level of discourse. Nachiketa said, 'When a man dies, there is this doubt: Some say, he is; others say, he is not. Taught by thee, I would know the truth. This is my third wish.'[27]

Understanding the thrust of the question, that Nachiketa is probing the fringes of an entire new spiritual world from that of the Vedic rites and might well be ready to enter it, Death parried with him. He went through the time-honored conventions of the master seeming to frustrate and discourage the novice in order to test him. He informed Nachiketa that the gods themselves find the answer hard to understand and urged him to select some other favor. He urged him to select sons, cattle, elephants, gold, a mighty kingdom, or celestial maidens so beautiful as not to be meant for mortals.

But Nachiketa stood fast, pointing out that these things are only grasped for a fleeting day, then vanish like smoke. In the process, they wear away the senses. How can one desire them, he asked Death, who has once seen Death's face? There is a secret of imperishability and immortality that is beyond them, he insisted, and he would not yield till Death had imparted it.

Inwardly well pleased, Death confirmed that there is another secret, one that cannot really be taught at all, but can be caught from a true teacher by the student who is truly prepared – that the Self within is the imperishable, changeless Brahman, the One beyond and, at the same time, in all these forms and changes. The mantra, or sound, that expresses Brahman himself, and whose recitation can give rise to his consciousness, is 'OM.' The King of Death continues:

> The Self, whose symbol is OM, is the omniscient Lord. He is not born. He does not die. He is neither cause nor effect. This Ancient One is unborn, imperishable, eternal: though the body be destroyed, he is not killed.
>
> If the slayer think that he slays, if the slain think that he is slain, neither of them knows the truth. The Self slays not, nor is he slain.
>
> Smaller than the smallest, greater than the greatest, this Self forever dwells within the hearts of all. When a man is free from desire, his mind and senses purified, he beholds the glory of the Self and is without sorrow.
>
> Though seated, he travels far; though at rest, he moves all things. Who but the purest of the pure can realize this Effulgent Being, who is joy and who is beyond joy.
>
> Formless is he, though inhabiting form. In the midst of the fleeting he abides forever. All-pervading and supreme is the Self. The wise man, knowing him in his true nature, transcends all grief.
>
> The Self is not known through study of the scriptures, nor through subtlety of the intellect, nor through much learning; but by him who longs for him is he known. Verily unto him does the Self reveal his true being.
>
> By learning, a man cannot know him, if he desist not from evil, if he control not his senses, if he quiet not his mind, and practice not meditation.[28]

This eternal self is clearly the answer to a deeper level of question than how to gain a temporary heaven through spiritual technology, through the manipulation of cosmic forces inner and outer. Nachiketa's final question made a more philosophical inquiry: in effect, is there that within a human being which is one with timeless reality itself, and not subject of the vicissitudes of space and time. Here is another level of Axial Age query, one which had implications for the great issues of personal and historical afterlife meaning. It eventuates in the last of the tensions regarding afterlife belief we listed in the first chapter: the One vs. the many, ultimate absorption in the One vs. remaining as one among the many on their winding paths through life and death. To this issue we will return.

Chapter 3

The Several Homelands of the Heart: Abodes of the Soul

China and the Afterlife

If there be an afterlife, the next question would naturally be, where does the spirit (or whatever remains) of the deceased go? On this point there are virtually as many answers as imaginable postmortem destinies, and in some cases more than one soul abides in a single individual so that diverse aspects of self, and various sites of continuing after-death life, can be accommodated. Take the example of traditional China.

Do you ever feel that there are two persons within you, one lofty, benevolent, interested in spiritual things and inclined toward them; the other far more focused on the material body, its appetites and desires? One the spirit of day and the mountaintops, the other of night and the valley? In traditional China these would have been the *hun* and *po* souls. The *hun* soul is associated with yang energy, that of sun and sky, high ground, the masculine, rulership, the dragon and the first half of the year, the time of growth and increasing light. The *po* soul is associated with yin, feminine energy, expressed in valleys, night, earth, the mysterious second half-year of harvest moon and gathering in.[29]

After death, the latter, the *po* soul resides in the grave, and can become an evil ghost if not suitably placated by proper burial and offerings. But the *hun*, containing characteristics of the *shen* or gods, will, it is hoped, become an ancestral spirit watching benevolently over his progeny in coming generations. Ancestors dwell in three places: in tablets in the home, at the grave, and in a 'lineage temple' maintained by the deceased's extended family. The lineage temple can be a quite impressive edifice. Entering it, one is confronted with several tiers representing seven successive generations back, each bearing large tablets inscribed with the name of each male ancestor, generation upon generation, twice as many of course on each higher tier than the one below. One gains a powerful sense of the weight of ancestors looking down on one's life today, just as one enjoys a feeling of intimacy with them in the attractive spring and autumn ceremonies of cleaning the cemetery graves and eating a picnic in communion with those familiar souls.

The living are expected to care for the deceased in their parental line, as a payment of the debt one owes them, starting with the gift of life itself, which being of infinite worth can never be repaid in full. Yet, by worshiping ancestral spirits, the living also hope for boons of the sort those now looking down on them with spirit eyes should know how much their hardworking descendants would appreciate: wealth, rich harvests, progeny.[30]

One might wonder what the state of ancestral spirits in their own other world is like. From the point of view of Buddhism with its Axial Age afterlife individualism, as powerful a force in popular Chinese culture as ancestrism, even mighty progenitors are not exempt from suffering the results of their own karma, and like anyone else may undergo hideous punishment in the hells before assuming their rightful place in home and temple, or undergoing appropriate reincarnation.

Yet at the same time, it is acknowledged that while the world of ancestral shades is invisible to us mortals, it is nonetheless a realm that interpenetrates ours. There, the watchful soul's continuing life can be pleasant if he is supplied by his fleshly family with adequate offerings of food, housing, clothing, and money. These goods, including elaborate paper houses and huge wads of imitation paper money, could be bought in every traditional Chinese town, and were burned at the funeral and subsequent memorial occasions.

However, if, as sometimes happens, the deceased has no descendants, or they are too poor or uncaring to provide such goods, his state on the other side becomes more and more degraded, and in his rage he may attack the living, turning into a vicious ghost. Many are the stories of family members, often a young daughter, who saw a vision of such a neglected ancestor emaciated and in tatters, with angry glowing eyes, and who then begged the clan, out of pity and fear alike, to rectify the situation with fresh offerings.[31]

An interesting consequence of Chinese afterlife belief and of importance of family lineage is 'spirit marriage.' A girl who dies unmarried is in an unfortunate situation, since it is through marriage she acquires her true lasting identity, and it is at the household shrine of her husband's family that her ancestral tablet is maintained. Thus, sometimes the spirit of such an unmarried daughter will appear in a dream to her family, and ask to be married.

How does one find a groom for a ghost-bride? One trick is to place 'bait' in the form of a red envelope, customarily used in China for gifts of money, in the middle of a road as a likely young man approaches. Family members of the distressed spirit hide along the wayside. When the youth stops to pick up the seeming prize, they rush out to tell him he is the selected mate of a bride in the other world. If he refuses, he will be liable to the supernatural vengeance of which a rejected lover is capable. But if he accepts, he will of course be eligible for the dowry, which if bountiful might go far to alleviate his reluctance. A wedding ceremony similar to any other is held, save that the bride is represented only by her ancestral tablet. The groom's family is then obligated to provide her tablet regular offerings as though she had become a daughter-in-law in life.

Sometimes the young unmarried female spirit goes beyond dreams to express her unhappiness by means of sending sickness and other blights to her own family, until by divination and seances the cause of her distress is learned, and a suitable living husband is located for the sorrowing shade. There is even a goddess believed to specialize in such arrangements, her advice being communicated through mediums.[32]

The penetration of Buddhism into China in the early centuries C.E. made the situation even more complex. Buddhism added, as we have seen, enhanced individualism in its teaching about karma and rebirth in various realms to the family and tribal cohesion characteristic of earlier ancestrism. Chinese Buddhism taught that the deceased are individually judged by the fearsome Yen-lo (the Chinese version of Yama, King of the Dead, whom we met as Nachiketa's host in the Katha Upanishad), who metes out to each his or her karmic deserts. The departed spirit could be sent to any of the six realms of rebirth already mentioned: those of the gods, humans, asuras or incessantly fighting warriors, animals, hungry ghosts, or hell-beings. Yet all this was accommodated to Confucian ancestral spirits, including spirit-brides, and Taoist earthly as well as heavenly immortality.

Home Souls and Wandering Souls

The concept of at least two souls per individual is far from unique to China. Most native American people believed in one soul linked to home, hearth, breath, and life in this world, which dies with the body; and another, called a free soul, capable of wandering away from the body in dreams or visions. It may even visit distant lands or the abode of the dead, there meeting deceased ancestors. But on such ventures a soul may become lost, strayed, or stolen; a disaster like this can lead to sickness or even death.

The Sioux spoke of four souls. Three of them died with the individual's physical death. The fourth could be maintained in a kind of bundle, containing hair of the deceased reverently wrapped in valuable skins, and placed off the ground on a tripod inside a tipi. Offerings of buffalo meat and wild cherry juice, the Sioux's most sacred food and drink, were presented before this shrine on behalf of all creatures, 'two-legged, four-legged, and flying,' to Wakan Tanka, the mysterious force behind the universe, to the Four Winds, and to Mother Earth. The food substances would then be consumed by four virgins, so that something of the soul's power would be transmitted through them to a new generation when the time came for them to give birth. After a suitable time, this soul would be released. The bundle would be carried outdoors and its spirit-dweller let go to commence its great journey onward, with the admonition to 'always look back upon your people that they may walk the sacred path with firm steps.'[33]

Further insight into soul-concepts can be gained from scenarios of the recovery of vagrant souls. Among the Salish natives of the United States and Canadian Pacific Northwest, this task was accomplished by several shamans together. After drumming, chanting, and feasting in the presence of the sick person, they made as if they were traveling to the Land of the Dead in a boat, imitating paddling. Along the way these specialists in the sacred crossed their legs like the dead, and hunted and fished as though they were denizens of that place, as it were to fool its ghostly guardians. Nonetheless they have to overcome obstacles: a raging torrent, angry spirits who try to keep them from entering. In tremendous struggles, including throwing burning torches, which greatly enhance the drama of the performance, the heroic shamans enter the other world. In time they find the lost soul and return bearing it, being careful to close the door to the Land of the Dead behind them. As they sail triumphantly back, they sing the song of the recovered soul. One can well imagine that after observing such a noble battle on his behalf, and now hearing the song of his own soul, the ailing individual would feel tremendously heartened.[34]

This scenario clearly presupposes a picture of the other world concretely realized, and not very different from this world. That was indeed the case with most Native Americans. The Thompson River people, or Nlaka'pamux, of British Columbia, part of the Salish group of tribes, affirmed that the Land of the Dead is toward the sunset, and to reach it one has to pass through a dim twilight region. The trail winds round and round, though there is a straight short cut used by shamans. As one gets closer to the other world, the way becomes smoother and lighter. One passes a huge pile of clothes left by venturers from the land of the living, for they are not needed here.

One must then encounter three stern, elderly guardians whose task is to send back those not yet ready for this land. Those who successfully pass them find their spirits rising, for they soon arrive at a warm, sunny, smiling realm of abundant grasses, sweet-smelling flowers, and ripe berries. At its heart is a great hall with many cheery fires, and within people are heard laughing, singing, beating drums, and preparing to welcome their new guest. All are naked but make nothing of it. They are delighted to greet the newcomer, and carry him on their shoulders.[35]

Indeed, for many people, the afterlife is little more than a presumably improved version of life here. The Inuit (Eskimos) conceive of it as including prosperous fishing; for some Native Americans, the afterworld was well stocked with buffalo; Germanic warriors continued fighting in Valhalla as here below; other stories envision the departed planting rice, felling trees, carrying on commerce and family life as before, but perhaps more happily.[36] According to the Ainu of northern Japan, the other world was opposite to ours, so that when it was night here it was day there. But the other world was more blissful and eternal, being home to the *kamui*, or gods; some say all the deceased become *kamui*. Communication between the two realms is possible: through dreams, and in the form of ghosts, who are the dead come back as messengers. It is also possible through animal spirits, as in the famous Ainu bear sacrifice, when a bear cub is lovingly raised, then sacrificed and commissioned to carry a petition for continued blessings to heaven.[37]

But, as we shall see, there is also a radically different theocentric view, especially associated with the Axial Age religion, insisting all that is set aside, and the deceased are engaged in the far more worthy occupation of worshiping God or enjoying mystical union with the divine, or else in undergoing grievous punishment. First, however, more about spirits whose world seems more continuous with ours.

Ancestral Spirits

Sometimes the souls of the deceased, even if of the wandering kind, maintain a relationship with the living. Among the Luguru of East Africa, for example, the *mitsimu* or spirits of grandparents play a very active role in a person's life. They are guardians of the traditional moral law, as might be expected, yet as invisible actors they also add a note of the marvelous and miraculous to everyday life. The appearance of omens, such as a solitary unusual animal, is ascribed to them. Their presence is particularly felt in awe-inspiring places: burial grounds, deep lakes, waterfalls. Yet they can also bring sickness or other disaster when one is in need of punishment. These numinous spirits are independent powers in the Luguru's pluralistic universe; while the high god, Mulungu, created the universe, he is not ordinarily addressed or concerned with worldly affairs, but leaves them in the hands of humans living and ancestral.

On moral issues, the ancestors are generally aligned with one's maternal uncles, who in this matrilineal society are the real authorities. One Luguru informant put it this way:

> Or suppose you want to go to Dar es Salaam [the major city in the area], and you ask permission from your maternal uncle and he says, 'You can't go!' and you say 'I'm going!' and then he says, 'All right, you'll see for yourself!' Then where you are going there is sure to turn out some danger. From the *mitsimu*.[38]

Among the Kgaga, a Sotho tribe in southern Africa, similar belief in the guardianship and power of ancestral spirits obtains, but with special emphasis on the way one's four grandparents, both paternal and maternal, work together as a team. After burial, the spirit of the deceased ancestor is brought back to the home in a special ritual, and housed in the family shrine. On the other hand, these protectors do not actively live on past two or three generations, but fade out as they are replaced by more recent ancestors.[39]

Here, as in China and much of the traditional world generally, ancestral spirits are vital, active forces in the lives of the descendants.

Their 'place,' in other words, is not far away, but here, invisibly at our sides, in reality at the cause of much which happens to us, ultimately for our good.

When the soul is twofold, as we have already seen in the Chinese case, that duality can account for both a remote afterlife and the ongoing ancestral presence. Among the Langalanga, Melanesian people in the Solomon Islands who follow a life of fishing and tuber agriculture, two circulating spirits are recognized, the *agalo* and the *kwasi*. Of these two souls, the *agalo* remains around the village, even as the skull is kept there in a special temple; the *kwasi* goes to an island on the east end of Guadacanal. That island off the horizon is the Langalanga paradise, but it is not much different from the world the deceased left. Its inhabitants do what these people do normally, build houses, till gardens, and fish, but they have no contact with relations back in their former world.

An *agalo*, on the other hand, becomes an ancestral spirit. It receives much attention and worship, and can speak through mediums to the living. If such an ancestor feels neglected, his spirit can cause sickness or trouble. In this circumstance, the medium will usually report that the spirit wants a pig. This animal will then be sacrificed, and an ancestor's name called out with each twist of the rope used to strangle the victim. At the same time, those in the society who are powerful sorcerers are believed to derive their powers from the ancestors; so also do the quasi-divine sharks in the bay, thought to be special protectors and by some to be the spirits of very remote ancestors; offerings are made to them of the entrails of the slaughtered pigs.[40]

Yet another concept occurred on Yap in the South Pacific. It was said that after an individual has died, the soul remains around the burial site until the remains have decayed; only then is it light enough to ascend to heaven, where it dwells with the high god, Yalafath. But when it has been there long enough for its earthly odors to wear off, the spirit returns back to earth as a ghost, in which guise it may punish those who did not honor it sufficiently.[41]

It remains to add that belief in spirits, including vengeful ghosts, is by no means limited to the sort of societies that anthropologists traditionally study. Folklorists have collected innumerable examples from Europe, America, and elsewhere in the 'developed' world. An old man in Kentucky related that long ago two men who were mortal enemies got into a fight, and one stabbed the other fatally with a long, sharp knife. The narrator then reported that late one night he had to ride by the cemetery where the victim had been buried. As he came near it, his horse started bucking and became unmanageable. (Horses, he said, could always tell if a spirit or ghost was around.) He dismounted to see if he could determine what was wrong.

The intruder then saw a pale misty apparition rising from the part of the graveyard where the murdered man had been interred. It headed right toward him, and the horse ran off in panic. But finally the specter floated off in another direction, the mount calmed down, and the ride back home was completed.[42]

The dead, then, according to myth, folklore, and image, can return to visit our world. So they can also in numerous festivals when the veil between the two worlds is said to become thin, as on the Anglo-American Halloween (a descendant of the Celtic Samhain), or the Japanese Obon. But can humans in the midst of life visit the Land of the Dead?

Distant Shores

We have already mentioned horizontal cosmology, entailing belief that the Other World of the gods, the dead, the fairy folk, and of wonder lies not in the heavens above, but on the same plane as our earth, yet very far off, in the uttermost west or east. Nonetheless, very intrepid sailors may be able to navigate even such vast seas, or heroes explore beyond the farthest ranges to reach the mythic realm. Thus among the fabulous tales told of Alexander the Great, it is recounted that once in the far reaches of India he, with a few of his men, came to a land of darkness, and after passing through it emerged into a place less dark and of fragrant air. Crystal streams were abundant. The conqueror's cook washed a dried fish in one before preparing it for the table; the fish came to life, to the man's astonishment. The chef took a drink of those waters himself, and was fortunate enough to himself become immortal. Alas, Alexander later remarked, he himself did not drink of the waters of immortality when the opportunity was his.

Advancing further, they came to a holy field filled with light from neither sun, moon, nor stars, and encountered two strange white birds with human faces, which spoke in Greek. These marvelous avians warned the brave visitors to come no further, for the Realm of the Blessed was forbidden. Instead, Alexander would be given the kingdom of the Indian ruler Porus. After further adventures, including an attempt to capture the white birds, the Macedonian was forced to realize he must be content with conquering this earth; the land of immortality was not for him.[43]

Whether this wonderland was indeed a homeland of the dead, like those western islands of departed heroes, Elysium and the Hesperides, is not entirely clear, but is not unlikely. In any case, the notion of an incredibly distant yet barely accessible paradise is established. The same can be said of the marvelous journey tales of the Celtic people. In them, a realm of wonder is found very far out across the western sea, or in some cases underground. In extant stories, the fabulous shore is inhabited by folk neither gods nor the departed, but is a fairyland like those well known to folklore. But many scholars have suggested that in their pre-Christian form the far-voyagers may well have made visits to the Land of the Dead.

One of the most famous of these stories, recounted as *Preiddeu Annwfn* ('The Spoils of Annwfn'), ascribed to the great half-legendary Welsh poet Taliesin, centers on the much-celebrated King Arthur. In it, the bard sings of how that monarch, still young and full of arrogance, determined to sail to the farthest west and raid Annwfn (pronounced 'Annoovun'), the Land of Faerie.

Three ships set out toward the setting sun, running before brisk winds from the east into uncharted seas, beset with proud banners and mighty arms. Accompanying the ambitious ruler, the incomparable bard Taliesin was able to weave marvelous enchantments of song that could sustain the spirits of any army till victory was won. He was also no mean adept in the arts of real magic, for many were the tales of his shapeshifting, and his ability to sing the powers of nature itself into serving his ends. Also on board was Llwch Lleminawc, the world's mightiest warrior. Could Faerie itself withstand the world's noblest king, greatest bard, and mightiest warrior all at once?

In fact, the vainglorious expedition would learn that the Other World does not countenance challenges from mortals, however exalted in their own eyes. To be sure, the uninvited visitors learned much, but the lessons were both wonderful and bitter. Furthermore, they were veiled in mystery, so that when the words of Taliesin's song about the adventure were written down, they seemed sometimes to glow, and then sometimes to fade so as to be unreadable – a journey that wanted at once to be famous and forgotten.

They sailed and sailed, out beyond the horizons of this world, according to the bard. Finally they landed on the strand of a fog-shrouded twilight island, and above its mists there rose the towers of a mighty turreted castle of glass shimmering the light above the sea-haze.

Approaching the mysterious edifice, the party passed a silent senti-
nel, then came to a fountain from which wine continually bubbled,
and by it rested a cauldron guarded by nine maidens. (Maidens of
great beauty are frequently a part of tales of journeys to the earthly
paradise. In some cases the appealing woman appears to the hero on
the terrain of our world, promising him honor, reward, and perhaps
her love, if he will assist her in some battle or difficulty. The mortal
goes with the mysterious maid in all her glamor, perchance not to
return until after ages of our time, or perchance almost instant-
aneously. In the present tale, the fair ladies are not met till Annwfn is
attained, but they have a special role as protectors of its magic.)

Arthur and his men realized that this cauldron, no doubt related to
the Holy Grail, was a work of sorcery – good sorcery in the right
hands, but sorcery and therefore dangerous nonetheless. Its blue-
enameled contours, encrusted with pearls, radiated a power that
bestowed wisdom and enabled men to sing and fight with valor. The
invaders also understood that it provided food in abundance, but only
for the brave; cowards would find nothing in it for them.

The brash visitors wanted to steal the cauldron, and indeed carried it
as far as their camp. But then six thousand warriors of Annwfn came
forth and fought the invaders, killing all of them but seven, who alone
managed to return to Britain. Taliesin was among them, surviving to
tell the tale in his mysterious manner. He implied they were fortunate
to escape at all, for high in the glass fortress of this land of enchant
ment was a prison. There languished a Welsh king of old, Gweir, and
two other Welsh royal predecessors of Arthur, Pwyll and Pryderi,
father and son, who were now slaves in Annwfn. They had, like
Arthur, in their time tried to trespass into this forbidden land, and were
paying the eternal price of their imprudence.

Not only that, but penalty extended back to their home kingdoms,
for Annwfn has secret agents and mystic lines of influence throughout
this world. The realms of the imprisoned monarchs of old suffered
plague and famine at the same time their rulers were taken into perpetual duress, and Taliesin had no doubt that the growing misfortune
of Arthur's once-happy Camelot, by which that sovereign was
deceived by his queen and greatest knight, then finally killed by his
bastard son, was ultimately due to the disfavor of Annwfn and its
princes. Those otherworldly lords do not take insults to the sanctity of
their land lightly, and their vengeance though sometimes slow is sure.[44]

Although, in the half-Christianized poetry of Taliesin, Annwfn is not
exactly the Land of the Dead, the presence there of three kings long

dead in this world may hint at an earlier status. In any case, it offers a stunning example of the Other World of horizontal cosmology, in which its denizens dwell in a place that may be reached from here though with great difficulty, and which extends its sway for good or ill into our earth, but which possesses a jealously-watched security of its own.

The perilous pilgrimage to the Other World may have also been acted out on this earth in ancient Britain. In the summer of 2009, a surprising discovery was unearthed only a mile from the famous Stonehenge monument – the remains of another megalithic stone circle, called Bluehenge. The theory has been advanced that these two neolithic temples, together with another of timber posts 1.2 miles northeast of Stonehenge up the Avon River, could have been stages in a solemn funeral journey. The dead might have first brought to Woodhenge, then ritually brought down the Avon, the stream being a symbol of the passage from life to death. They would then brought ashore in Bluehenge, whose small impressive circle represented death, and finally carried up the 1.8 miles of the 'avenue' from that edifice to Stonehenge, aligned with the summer solstice and perhaps representing entry into the world of the Afterlife.[45]

Grottoes of Earth and Heaven

Returning to China, let us consider the *xian* or 'immortals' of Taoism. They present still another possibility, that of one who has not passed through death to newness of life, but who have gone directly from worldly life to eternal life without physically dying. These colorful individuals, the subject of countless works of art and fairytale-like stories, continue to live on in 'grottoes,' hidden recluses either in this world or in heaven. Particularly famous for its population of immortals is the realm of the Queen-Mother of the West, Xi-wang-mu, who according to legend even came out of her remote palaces in the Kunlun mountains back to the Middle Kingdom to instruct emperors on longevity. No less celebrated is that seaward abode of immortals, the island of Penglai off the east coast of China.

These fabulous places were sought by bold travelers; even a glimpse of the Blessed Land might be enough to secure one a place therein. So hoped the first emperor of the Qin dynasty who, not content with unifying the vast empire (221 B.C.E.), paced eagerly along the eastern seaboard, eyes eager for even a glimmer of the strand of Penglai where grew the peaches of immortality. Yet immortals might be found any-where. The famous Eight Immortals (one of them a woman), com-monly portrayed in a boat sailing to Penglai, also appeared on the streets of ordinary cities, often anonymously, as beggars, officials, actors, and pilgrims.

How does one become an immortal? The basic method is through Taoist yoga, which in brief means meditation by which the *qi* ('chi') or life-energy is circulated around the body with the help of posture and breathing exercises, cleansing the fleshly vehicle and removing all barriers to the right balance of yin and yang (feminine and masculine energies), and the five elements; death comes from their disharmony. Diet is also important; Taoist adepts eliminate meat, the 'five grains,' and other foodstuffs till they may be living, allegedly, on nothing but dew, powdered mother-of-pearl, and moonbeams, together with the sacred peaches of immortality that grow in the paradises beyond set-ting sun and rising moon. Alchemical elixirs of immortality likewise offered assistance in the process. Sexual yoga was also practiced by Taoists: one could attain the desired balance of yin and yang by absorbing sufficient fluids of the other gender.

Yet the process of becoming an immortal, with the various ranks and powers available to them, could also involve aid that was undeni-ably magical. The early Taoist writer Huainanzi (179–122 B.C.E.), describing the court of the Queen Mother, with its ranks of immortal courtiers and its delightful happiness, tells of three parks, 'Hanging Garden,' 'Cool Wind,' and 'Enclosed Park of Paulownias,' all contain-ing golden ponds of cinnabar water, a drink bestowing immortality. Each also contains a peak; climbing the first also makes one immortal, the second in addition makes one a magical being with power over wind and rain, while the third enables one to ascend to heaven and become a divinity in the palace of the emperor of heaven.[46]

Immortals, then, like the dead generally, can be both near and far away. Can they also circulate between this world and highest heaven through rebirth and reincarnation? We shall next examine that issue.

Chapter 4

*Circling Paths, Endless Journey:
Reincarnation vs. Eternal Life in
Heaven or Hell*

Coming Back to What You Want

The previous chapter dealt primarily with afterlife images based on horizontal cosmology in preliterate or folk religion. The Land of the Dead was far across the sea or beyond distant mountain ranges, or at least in a nearby underworld or heaven, but basically on the same plane of reality, and in the same kind of reality, as you or me. Yet occasionally hints of something else present themselves: souls might also proceed to a faraway Dreamtime of the gods and of the departed, and then after a limited time in another place return to the former home to be reborn once again in human form. These two pictures, reincarnation in this or another realm, or eternal life eternally beyond this world, suggestions or parts of popular belief before, became more rigorously defined doctrinally in the Axial Age religions of the Founders, with their relatively more sophisticated intellectual structures.

Perhaps the earliest scriptural texts to teach reincarnation clearly are the Upanishads, the last and most philosophical of the Vedas sacred to Hinduism. The Brihadaranyaka Upanishad tells us that, 'As a leech, having reached the end of a blade of grass, takes hold of another blade and draws itself to it, so the Self, having left this body behind it unconscious, takes hold of another body and draws himself to it.'[47] The same text goes on to inform us that this next body is one in accordance with his desire: not his fanciful wishes, of course, but those desires truly expressed by his deeds, his way of life. In reincarnation you get what you want, as shown by the sum of your thoughts, words, and deeds; then you have to live with it.

As a man's desire is, so is his destiny. For as his desire is, so is his will; as his will is, so is his deed; and as his deed is, so is his reward, whether good or bad.

A man acts according to the desires to which he clings. After death he goes to the next world, bearing in his mind the subtle impressions of his deeds; and after reaping there the harvest of his deeds, he returns again to this world of action. Thus he who has desire continues subject to rebirth.[48]

In the Katha Upanishad, cited earlier, Death himself tells Nachiketa:

To the thoughtless youth, deceived by the vanity of earthly possessions, the path that leads to the eternal abode is not revealed. *This world alone is real; there is no hereafter* – thinking thus, he falls again and again, birth after birth, into my jaws.[49]

In other words, if one acts as though what she or he really wants is to be reincarnated, to have another go at life in this world of light and shadow, of actions and reaction (karma), she or he will find herself in the body of a newborn baby, generally forgetful of previous lives, but in a situation in which unresolved issues – unfulfilled dreams, unresolved relationships, attachments, addictions, all that could go under the general category of desires – will present themselves again, no doubt in new forms but no less insistent, until they are truly left behind.

Indeed, the Upanishads inform us that a dreamlike intermediate state exists between lives. In this state one lives only in the 'subtle body, on which are left the impressions of his past deeds, and of these impressions he is aware, illumined as they are by the light of the Self.' Thus in this state, as in a kind of do-it-yourself forum, one experiences again crucial events of his former life, and also, 'while in the intermediate state, he foresees both the evils and the blessings that will yet come to him, as these are determined by his conduct, good and bad, on the earth.' While these foreshadowing are 'real' only in the sense that nocturnal dreams are real, they are no less significant as indicators of the state of one's soul and destiny.[50]

The reel of dreams can, however, be run out, leaving only clear light. We are told no less assuredly, 'But he in whom desire is stilled suffers no rebirth. After death, having attained to the highest, desiring only the Self [the atman, one's true nature, one with Brahman], he goes to no other world. Realizing Brahman, he becomes Brahman.'[51]

Other ancient Hindu sources were more explicit about possible fates via reincarnation. *The Laws of Manu* (composed c. 200 B.C.E.–200 C.E.) specifies numerous destinies in which the punishment clearly fits the crime: those who delight in hurting others become carnivorous animals, who steal grain become rats, who steal meat vultures, who eat forbidden food worms, and so on through scores of categories.[52] On the other hand, for good karma one can enter the kingdoms of the gods or angelic beings.

Several important ancient philosophers of the west, all broadly contemporary with the composition of the Upanishads, seem to have affirmed some form of reincarnation or metempsychosis (the transmigration of the soul among different forms of life), or were at least prepared to experiment with the idea. Pythagoras (fl. c. 455 B.C.E.) reportedly professed the doctrine, and recognized the soul of a deceased friend in the body of a dog that was being beaten.

The great Plato (427–327 B.C.E.) taught in the Phaedrus that the soul is reborn in a new body suitable to the level of truth it has realized, saying that the soul which has seen highest truth finds birth as a philosopher, artist, musician, or lover; next highest as a righteous king or warrior; and so down the scale. At the end of *The Republic*, Plato tells his myth of Er, a warrior who has been left for dead but then had what amounts to a near-death experience (NDE). When he returned to the living after ten days, he reported he has seen the souls of the departed selecting which of available lives they would take for their next birth, and drawing lots to determine in what order they got to choose. But the choice was inevitably in accordance with the candidate's own wisdom or folly. Some even opted for an animal experience: Orpheus, with his love of beauty, fixed on the life of a swan, the mighty warriors Ajax and Agamemnon appropriately chose lion and eagle, respectively. But with Plato one can never be quite sure when he is presenting what he himself believed literally, and when only provocative fables or fictions by which he hoped to stimulate thought or get a good argument going.

Plotinus (204–269 C.E.), the father of Neoplatonism, in *The Descent of the Soul* proposed that the soul is educated through a series of births in a material body, in which the lesson above all is to recognize the superiority of spiritual nature. Neoplatonism came to have a profound influence on subsequent Jewish, Christian, and Islamic theology and mysticism, although reincarnation was affirmed only in highly esoteric forms of the Abrahamic faiths, most notably Kabbalistic Judaism. Undoubtedly, however, these western precursors of modernity, along with heightened contact between the East and West in recent centuries, helped prepare the way for modern interest in the doctrine.[53]

Reincarnation Now

Reincarnation has enjoyed a remarkable revival in the nominally Judeo-Christian, western world since the mid-twentieth century. Once the position of only a few dissidents, plus certain Kabbalistic Jews, in a 2005 Harris poll 21% of Americans polled said they believed in reincarnation.[54] This belief was certainly given impetus by the celebrated 1960s counterculture's vogue for Eastern spirituality. But even before then, credit should be given to a 1956 bestseller that created such a furore it can virtually be considered a modern myth: that is, narrative which expresses in story form a worldview into which one can fit one's own life-story to give it enhanced meaning. That book was *The Search for Bridey Murphy* by Morey Bernstein.[55]

The tale was this. In 1952 Morey Bernstein, a Colorado businessman and hypnotist, conducted six sessions of deep hypnotic regression with a neighbor, Virginia Burns Tighe (1923–1995; she is given the name Ruth Simmons in the book). The young housewife was reportedly taken back before her present birth to a previous life in Ireland as Bridey (Bridget) Murphy, born 1798, died 1864. The trance material produced a remarkable wealth of detail concerning her childhood in Cork, marriage to a barrister named Sean Brian McCarthy and subsequent move to Belfast, her house and domestic life, and finally her death and burial.

Needless to say, when the book became a sensation reporters rushed to Ireland to try to verify the material, while psychologists analyzed it and Mrs. Tighe's background for any clues as to subconscious influences. No record of a Bridey Murphy matching the dates and locations in Ireland was found, and a childhood neighbor of Irish descent named Bridie Murphy Corkell was located. On the other hand, the hypnotic material did contain information about nineteenth-century Irish geography, business firms, and ways of life that would not normally be known to a non-scholarly person like Virginia Tighe. Debate rolled back and forth.[56]

From the point of view of myths and images of the afterlife, what is of most significance is the way Bridey Murphy sparked a rather sudden and dramatic upsurge of interest in, and for some belief in, reincarnation. Immediately after the publication of *The Search for Bridey Murphy* in 1956, the phenomenon produced a movie version as well as popular music recordings with titles like 'Do You Believe in Reincarnation?' 'The Love of Bridey Murphy,' and 'The Bridey Murphy Rock and Roll,' as well as at least one suicide, a teenager apparently wishing to enter the reincarnate life immediately. On a brighter note, the sale of virtually anything having to do with reincarnation boomed, and 'Come As You Were' parties were immensely popular.[57] The very successful 1965 musical, 'On a Clear Day You Can See Forever,' together with its 1970 movie version, also seems influenced by Bridey Murphy-type hypnotic regression.

In sum, a new (new to this culture) popular myth, in our meaning of the word, had taken hold, complete with paradigmatic model, multi-media reinforcement, and a general sense this is a view of the afterlife that is at once fun, voguish, and problem-solving in terms of understanding why one's life is the way it is. Over and over, one hears people say things like, 'I fear water because I died of drowning in a past life,' or 'That person makes me uneasy; I think it's because he and I had a bad marriage last time.' Opposition from powerful voices of both religious and scientific conventional wisdom was of course influential, and the majority was not convinced. Yet the force of a fresh modern myth/image, practically reified in the 'New Age' movement of the late twentieth century, could also be heard amid the party chatter and popular books and films.

Reincarnation or heaven and hell? Those who believe in the former say that rebirth in successive lives is more just, because it gives souls a chance to gradually learn and grow; for everything – even the possibility of an eternity in hell – to depend on just one life, in which one may have not possessed full information, or made foolish mistakes, is too harsh for a just God or universe. But those on the anti-reincarnation side argue that God is just though in ways sometimes past human understanding, and that reincarnation makes it too easy: one can always make excuses and say I'll do better next time; it is important to realize one's choices here and now, in the face of death and judgment, are immensely important, and opportunities once missed may not come again.

We will see that in Buddhism it is possible to have both reincarnation and heaven or hell.

Heavens Above, Hells Below

For many people of all religions, probably the first image to come to mind when the afterlife is mentioned is one of the traditional heaven: paradisal gardens of fountains and flowers, or the Heavenly Jerusalem with its streets of gold, to reward the righteous. Then may come an opposite image: the traditional hell, with its horrendous torture of those deserving punishment. For above all, heaven and hell bespeak righteous judgment and compensation for the vast inequities of this world. They establish that for which so many yearn, a sense of ultimate justice, and religions also teach of ways of access through faith and devotion to the place of repose even for those frail children of Earth unable to attain it otherwise.

Good examples are the Mahayana Buddhist Pure Lands, mentioned before. Heavenly waystations on the path to Nirvanic liberation: the Pure Lands of the great Buddhas, above all Amitabha (Amida in Japanese), are like auras of unimaginably powerful wisdom/energy surrounding mighty cosmic Buddhas and generated by their profound meditations, meditations that make and sustain universes. For us of human eyesight, those energies come into focus as fabulously gorgeous landscapes millions of miles across, strewn with flowers and gems common as gravel, music of unearthly beauty in the air.

Moreover, entry into ultimate Nirvana is easy from this realm – if it were not enough in itself – since no discordant distractions obtain to prevent those final meditations which open the way to release from all that is transitory, unsatisfactory, or ego-bound. On the other hand, because of Amida's ancient vow to bring, out of his infinite compassion, all who call upon his name in faith into his Pure Land, entry is accessible to all, rich or poor, educated or not, monk or layman. It was a matter not of merit by which one earned one's way into the Pure Land, but of the infinite grace of Amida Buddha, given freely to everyone.

The whole point is that liberation is not arduous, but surprisingly easy. Yet that easiness, paradoxically, makes it hard for some people. As in the case of bhakti Hindu or Christian salvation by faith or devotion (strictly, salvation by God's grace received through faith), the idea one could live a life of sin and then be saved at the last minute by a confession of faith does not sit well with critics. If all it takes is faith, what does that say about the effort some put into seeking out salvation with diligence, mortifying self to watch, pray, and do good works in season and out?

Those on the faith side respond that striving after salvation through effort or 'works' is precisely what is deceptive: one builds up one's ego even as one ostensibly tries to reduce ego, through pride in one's spiritual achievement. ('See what a great meditator or philanthropist I am! Surely I'll make it to heaven.') By trusting in the grace of another, Amida or Christ, one just lets go of ego, forgets about it, and then is free to love God and humanity not out of a calculating desire for recompense, but just for their own sake. In any case, in Buddhism the way of Amida is there for those animated by the path of faith, the practices of Zen or Theravada vipassana for those following the meditation way, and of rituals like the elaborate mudras and mantras (gestures and postures; chants) of Tibetan Buddhism (Vajrayana) or Shingon in Japan for those who discover them to hold the highest power of all.

Western Monotheism

The western monotheistic religions go in a different direction in several respects. First, ordinarily heaven, identified with the Beatific Vision or the immediate presence of God, is the supreme state, not a waystation on the road to something even greater. Second, hell, though not always considered eternal, is the opposite of heaven and in that sense just as real and ultimate in its own way. Third, after the eschatological event earth itself is renewed to become a place of paradise along with heaven (the 'new heaven and earth' of Isa. 65:17 and 66:22, and Rev. 21:1). This scenario also includes the 'resurrection of the body,' suggesting a radically different view of the body, the earth, indeed matter itself, than that of those for whom all things are forever transitory, and who say neither the physical body nor this particular universe are abiding homes for those on the great pilgrimage into unconditioned reality.

No doubt much remains here to be debated and defined philosophically, but from our point of view, that of image and myth, is clear that the western monotheisms, in their traditional forms, offer not only a different picture but a different 'feel' and 'tone' about the afterlife from those of the East: one far more concrete, material, one might even say 'earthy,' than the Eastern side. There even the heavens themselves can seem like fascinating ever-changing cinematic stories shined on a screen, until finally the film is run through and only clear white light remains.

Heaven and Hell in Western Monotheism: Judaism

We have already described the afterlife in Zoroastrianism, perhaps the earliest version of what was to become the western monotheistic pattern. We may now go on to Judaism. Jewish views of the afterlife need to be understood in terms of two basic values in Judaism: the importance of the earth and of life in this world; and an orientation toward history, including its ultimate consummation, as the source of human meaning. For that reason, views of human destiny fulfilled in some other tangential after-death world, such as heaven or hell, is relatively de-emphasized. Those, like many Christians, for whom what happens after one dies seems virtually to be the main point of religion, will find in Judaism a quite different perspective. There, it is community, the Jewish way of life, a historical legacy, and the challenge of making this world better that are most important.

At the same time, it seems evident that from the years of the Babylonian Exile (597–538 B.C.E.) on, when Jews had contact with Zoroastrian Persia, that its view of judgment, resurrection, and a new earth were influential. They fitted well the Jewish view of life in history as important, by giving it a completion and fulfillment which justified the many sufferings of God's people in this world now. Yet in the eyes of most independent scholars, and of many traditional Jewish teachers, there are few if any references to a positive individual life after death in the Hebrew scriptures. Prophets like Isaiah instead painted a brilliant picture of the ideal world at the end of time, when God would come in judgment and then enact a new and better creation:

> For behold, I create new heavens and a new earth; and the former things shall not be remembered or come into mind. But be glad and rejoice for ever in that which I create . . . The wolf and the lamb shall feed together, the lion shall eat straw like the ox; and dust shall be the serpent's food. They shall not hurt or destroy in all my holy mountain, says the Lord. (Is. 65)

Ezekiel provided a prototype of resurrection in the famous 'dry bones' passage.

> Thus says the Lord God: Behold, I will open your graves, and raise you from your graves, O my people; and I will bring you home into

the land of Israel . . . And I will put my Spirit within you, and you
shall live, and I will place you in your own land. (Dn. 37)

But while speculation about the resurrection and the life to come was
prevalent in the Hellenistic period, and messianic belief was certainly
common – common enough to give rise to the Christian movement –
the majority of learned rabbis were reticent on the subject. The third-
century Palestinian sage Yohanan bar Nappaha said, 'All the prophets
prophesied only about the days of the Messiah; but of the world
to come, "eye hath not seen it, O God." (Is. 64:4).' His Babylonian
contemporary Rav (Abba bar Ayyvu) was a bit more forthcoming:
'In the world to come, there is no eating, no drinking, no begetting
of children, no bargaining or hatred or jealousy or strife; rather the
righteous will sit with crowns on their heads and enjoy the effulgence
of the *shekhinah*, God's presence.'[58]

As there is no mandatory doctrine about the Afterlife in Judaism,
a diversity of opinions have surfaced. Early C.E. *merkebah* or 'chariot'
mysticism postulated a series of seven concentric spheres or heavens,
each one closer to the Divine and further from the material plane
than the one before, through which the mystic could ascend in spirit
on the analogy of the chariot God provided Elijah to take him up
from earth when his work was done.[59] Other Medieval rabbis disputed the nature of souls in the 'End of Days' after the coming of
the Messiah and the new creation. Some considered their existence
to be entirely spiritual, while others thought they would enjoy an
intensely physical/spiritual life on earth. But prevalent opinion saw
life after death as a kind of journey, in which the deceased might
encounter the pains of the grave, the angel of silence, Satan, Gehinom
(purgatory or hell), or Gan Eden, paradise. All this, the wise said, is
beyond human understanding, and can be rendered only in parable
and analogy.

Gehinom, sometimes Gehenna, though often translated hell, is not
a place of eternal punishment in the Christian sense. It is rather a
place of purification, usually not lasting more than twelve months,
after which the departed may ascend to Gan Eden, the New Eden
or Paradise.

Today, in Orthodox Judaism, the traditional tenet of the resurrection
of the body is maintained. Conservative Judaism generally keeps the
language of resurrection in the liturgy, though it may be interpreted
metaphorically rather than literally. Liberal Jews, in the Reform and
Reconstructionist tradition, usually emphasize the importance of a

full life in this world while maintaining an agnostic position on life after death.

Finally, it should be pointed out again that the notion of reincarnation, while not an essential tenet of traditional Judaism, has been widely held as a mystical belief. It is not mentioned in classical sources such as the Mishnah or Talmud, or standard doctrinal statements. But the books of the Kabbalah, Jewish mysticism, do teach *gilgul*, transmigration of souls, and so also does Hasidism, which generally regards the books of Kabbalah as sacred texts.[60] The idea of reincarnation was accepted by the Baal Shem Tov, the founder of Hasidism, and by many of his successors. It has found its way into Jewish folk belief and folklore, being present in much Yiddish literature. From our point of view, perhaps reincarnation could be thought of as a middle way between belief in one life only, and resurrection at the End of Days; it suggests a more natural and gradated way by which souls could advance to the paradisal age.

The Christian Heavens and Hells, Plus Purgatory

The Christian faith, now embracing about one third of the world's population at least in terms of cultural background, has presented several diverse, and not always completely consistent, views of the Afterlife. That is because of the different sources of belief that have gone into the religion, and because it has operated in different cultural eras.

Christianity was born from Judaism at a time when Judaism, having long suffered under alien empires, was awash with apocalyptic expectation of the end of the age, when an all-powerful Messiah would arrive to defeat Israel's enemies, restore the kingdom to Jerusalem, and bring in a new world of righteousness and plenty. Characteristically, apocalypticists envisioned upcoming 'war in heaven' between invisible beings both good and evil. Angels would battle alongside the messianic Promised One, and demons would war against the legions of light, for control of individuals and nations. Then, when the powers of good triumphed, those unjustly killed would be raised by God from the dead to enjoy the new age of God's rule. In some forms of apocalypticism, expectation also looked for universal resurrection, to be followed by a Great Judgment in which the wicked would be separated from the righteous. Christianity embraced such scenarios, as is evident in *The Book of Revelation* and numerous passages in the Gospels and Epistles.

But another early Christian theme, influenced by the Hellenistic mystery religions, Gnosticism, and later by Neoplatonism, focused on a divine light or spark hidden within each person. In this context, salvation was the overcoming of ignorance and alienation, until one fully realized the inner divinity's reunion with the Divine.

The Gospels, at least on the surface, favor the contemporary Jewish apocalyptic view of the Afterlife, as the result of resurrection of the dead in the context of the messianic war and victory. There are, however, traces of other perspectives. One of the few concrete pictures of the state of souls after death is the parable of the rich man and the beggar Lazarus, in which angels carry Lazarus to Abraham's bosom, while the rich man suffers thirst in a flaming hell, but is unable to receive even a drop of water from Lazarus because of the great gulf fixed between them. This image is perhaps not apocalyptic, but from older Jewish folk belief.

John's gospel, on the other hand, contains language that moves toward the Hellenistic image of a divine soul within that is awakened by the presence of Christ as Light in the world, to be received here and now by those who love the Light rather than darkness. But all the gospels are dominated by a new factor, decisive for Christians: the resurrection of Jesus in our own time, which is the truest warrant of all for the Afterlife, however conceived.

St. Paul in his epistles combines these ideas of spiritual warfare, resurrection, and individual eternal life in his own way. Jesus is the heavenly Lord to whom Christians are inwardly united, and whose life within each is immortal. Yet at Jesus' return deceased believers will rise and together with the living be drawn upward to meet him. *The Book of Revelation* greatly develops various of these themes, climaxing in a universal judgment. Books are opened containing a record of souls' deeds, and upon their contents an enthroned God makes his judicial decisions. The faithful will reign with God and Christ in a city with streets of gold and a paradisal garden, which is to come down from heaven. The wicked and the Devil will be cast into a lake of fire to suffer for their deeds.

As weeks, years, and centuries passed, and the apocalyptic return of Jesus failed to occur, interest moved toward individual judgment and reward or punishment, in effect after death, though formal belief in an ultimate General Resurrection and Last Judgment remained. The Virgin Mary and other saints were seen as pleading for the faithful at their judgment, and assisting them to reach heaven. Inevitably, it came to be felt that choice between immediate heaven and hell after personal death was too stark; some needed only more purification before entry into the realm of the blessed. So it was that the idea of Purgatory developed. Purgatorial suffering was the hard but passable road traversed by the vast number of mid-level souls.

Although not formally defined until the Councils of Lyons and Florence in the Middle Ages, the purgatorial concept appears in St. Augustine and, most interestingly, in the sixth century collection of NDEs collected by Pope Gregory the Great. An example is cited in the first chapter of this book. Here one finds guides, angels and demons, souls in places of purgation or hells fiery or cold, journeys through darkness, flowering meadows, borderlines, music, supernal light. Anxious individuals face records of their deeds in open books, and subsequently – for those who return from an otherworldly Near-Death state – the awesome experience may result in a transformed life. Overall, early medieval accounts tend to be somber, with great emphasis on the precariousness of salvation, the tremendous battle waged for each soul between angels and demons, and much stress on purgation and punishment in contrast to the occasional glimpses of heaven.

As the Middle Ages advanced, views of the Afterlife were tempered by the development of devotionalism, in which intense love between the worshiper and the figure of Jesus or Mary or another of the saints, seen as heavenly advocate, added both warmth and a certain reassurance to faith in the world to come. On the other hand, the Black Death and other calamities in the late Middle Ages led to much fearful preoccupation with death, purgatory, and hell. Abetting the anxiety was a 'forensic' or legalistic view of judgment. In trepidation over whether one had what was required to pass that great assize successfully, not surprisingly many sought to gain additional help in the form of indulgences or merit acquired by such acts as pilgrimage or extra devotions.

On the other hand, the doctrine of Purgatory alleviated to no small measure the uttermost levels of anxiety, as it allowed for those who were far from sainthood and not fully ready for heaven, but had no unabsolved mortal sins, which would send them to hell, to be purged or purified until they eventually reached the perfect state. Jacques Le Goff, in his *The Birth of Purgatory*, sets the explicit emergence of this concept in the half-century 1150–1200, though of course earlier theological developments led up to it. Assuming that after death the soul entered into a kind of waiting state until the last day and its final assignment to heaven or hell, Purgatory meant that time need not be wasted: '[S]omething new may happen to a human being between his death and resurrection. It offers a second chance to attain eternal life.'[61]

The purifying process in this intermediary other world was not necessarily pleasant. Its cleanings were mainly wrought by fire, and indeed no less an authority than Thomas Aquinas opined that the flames of Purgatory were a thousand times more painful than any on earth. Yet Purgatory was not everlasting; hope lay at the end, as in the karmic Buddhist hells. The 'poor souls' suffer purging fires for a long or short time, until they have been cleansed of evil, justice is satisfied, and they can then await entry into the presence of God. Moreover, the purgatorial sentence could be shortened by the prayers and spiritual aid of the living, including pilgrimages, mortifications, and donations made on behalf of the penitents in that third place.

Closely related to purgatorial sentencing was the doctrine of Indulgences. The Pope, it was believed, held the spiritual key to a 'treasury of merit' – the superabundance of merit attained by Christ and the saints. Indulgences were certificates issued by the Pope, the effect of which was to transfer to the petitioner certain quantities of this merit. The document affirmed that because the recipient had done an adequate number of acts of penitence and devotion, so many 'days' – or possibly all (plenary indulgence) – of his or her prospective suffering in purgatory had been remitted. Indulgences could be obtained for oneself or, as in the case of the compassionate aid just mentioned, by one person on behalf of another, living or dead.

This doctrine was not without its attractive side. It was a concrete way of stating the benefits accrued from such extra and innocent religious acts as pilgrimage, and it suggested, in the exchange of merit idea, that Christians deeply share in one another's lives. At its best such charitable labors on their behalf could be seen as following the biblical admonition to bear one another's burdens (Gal. 6:2), and indeed in that light was an implementation of the communion of saints. Indulgences are still made available in the Roman Catholic Church.

But in the days of Martin Luther, on the eve of the Protestant Reformation, indulgences were being widely distributed in Germany with, in the eyes of the great reformer and other German observers, little consideration but for the donation of money customarily given by the recipient. In effect, they were being used as a means of church fund-raising, and a special drive was on to raise funds for the building of St. Peter's Basilica in Rome. Moreover, the theology behind indulgences went very much counter to Luther's new inner discovery of salvation by grace through faith only, based only on the Bible.

So it was that the Protestant reformation rejected Purgatory and the role of the saints, leaving only heaven or hell. The concepts of the two opposing destinations were not much modified, however, nor was the forensic image of judgment leading to one or the other. The great anxiety that such a situation could impose on one who took it seriously was somewhat mitigated by Protestant ideas of faith and grace. For Luther, though one was a sinner, one could still be saved by sincere faith in the work of Christ; for Calvin, God's irresistible grace assured ultimate salvation to those called to be saved. Nonetheless gold and red-black images of two starkly opposed prospects, and the awesome judgment that would decide which way one's soul would fly, remained to haunt the believer's mind. We will look further at Reformation ideas, and subsequent developments in popular Christianity, in the next chapter.

The Paradise of Islam

Like all the monotheistic religions, Islam emphasizes a highly contrasted heaven and hell. The Prophet said, 'When we live, we dream, and when we die, we wake' – to our true eternal nature and eternal life. If Muslim, to what would you awake?

Heaven or paradise is actually seven heavens, progressively further and further from the material world, so that the seventh is in the presence of the sun-like brightness of God as comprehended by mystic vision. The concept is probably derived from pre-Kabbalistic Jewish 'chariot mysticism,' which based mystical ascent through seven spheres on the upward journey of Elijah's chariot; it no doubt also lies behind the Prophet Muhammad's famous Night Journey, when he was taken from the site of the Temple in Jerusalem to the highest heaven.

One might have expected a desert people, like the first Muslims, to see heaven as a glorious version of the oases for which they yearned out under the hot sun and on hard dry terrain, and so it was. Paradise was al-Jannah, the Garden (a term also used for the Garden of Eden). Enclosed against storm, cooled and watered by sparkling streams and fountains, abounding in fruit, this divine estate was a place of rest and delight. Eternal male and female companions welcomed the righteous; the houris or female attendants are said by staider commentators to represent spiritual states of rapture.

As for hell, sophisticated Islamic writers, ancient and modern, view hell less in terms of divine punishment, despite images of fire and

sometimes of tremendous pressure, than as a reminder of the con-
suming chaos and inner tension of a life in denial of God, the one
Reality, and so also negation of who one truly is, as a creature of God.
The question as whether hell is eternal is left open, though classical
theologians have tended to feel that one who was so chaotic and torn
apart by the contradiction between perverse belief, or unbelief, and
actual reality would only deteriorate further into nothingness rather
than come out whole and alive.

Yet the possibility remains; there is a Hadith (reported saying of the
Prophet) that 'He shall make men come out of hell after they have been
burned and reduced to cinders.' And another Hadith says: 'Those who
have merited paradise will enter it; the damned will go to hell, God will
then say; Let those leave hell whose hearts contain even the weight of a
mustard seed of faith: Then they will be released, although they have
already been burned to ashes, and plunged into the river of rain-water,
or into the river of life; and immediately they will be revived.'

Muslim teachers also offer the hopeful possibility of a purgatorial
state for those who are not ready for paradise, but open to further
purification after death. Although not mentioned in the Qur'an, theologians have taken lines such as the foregoing to suggest the probability
of an intermediate state, or at least a non-eternal purification in hell,
for those who are able to make use of it: al-Barzakh, to be discussed
later. By the same token, teachers take it that children who die before
the age of reason will be saved in paradise.

Above all, Islam teaches the presence of God, the all-consuming
Reality without a second, everywhere: Whichever way one looks,
there is the Face of God, says the Qur'an. But whether one receives
it as the cool calm or paradise or the fires of hell depends upon one's
own inner state.[62]

The Near-Death Experience

Finally, let us return to present-day images of the afterlife as endless
journey. An important example of what might be considered a modern
myth of the afterlife – myth in the sense of stories into which our own
lives can be inserted and interpreted, not in the sense of untrue – is the
NDE, as important now as in the days of Plato or Pope Gregory.

Many of us undoubtedly know, from accounts told to us by others,
from reading, perhaps even from personal experience, of unusual
events happening to people who have approached the gates of death,

or been 'clinically dead' in a hospital or accident situation, and then underwent a profound alteration of consciousness. Some have reported seeing a bright welcoming light that is also a loving Presence, though occasionally harsh light or darkness. Many have encountered welcomers, perhaps deceased friends, relatives, angels, or religious figures.

There may also occur a 'life review,' not always pleasant, in which one sees all of one's life pass by; a few have had an empathic life review, not only seeing but *re-experiencing* their lives, with an expanded consciousness that includes all the effects they had on other sentient beings, even the 'ripple effect' of knowing third- and fourth-hand the impacts on still other beings, of what one has lovingly, carelessly, or callously inflicted on others.

Kenneth Ring defined the 'core experience' of an NDE as typically including tremendous peace, a sense of being separate from the body, of moving through a dark space toward a beautiful light, a panoramic life review, and a decision or command to return to the body in this case. Here is an account of the light, from Raymond Moody's 1975 book, *Life After Life*, which initiated the recent interest in NDEs of the Light:

> I got up and walked into the hall to go get a drink, and it was at that point, as they found out later, that my appendix ruptured. I became very weak, and I fell down. I began to feel a sort of drifting, a movement of my real being in out of my body, and to hear beautiful music. I floated on down the hall and out the door onto the screened-in porch. There, it almost seemed that clouds, a pink mist really, began to gather around me, and then I floated right straight on through the screen, just as though it weren't there, and up into this pure crystal clear light, an illuminating white light. It was beautiful and so bright, so radiant, but it didn't hurt my eyes. It's not any kind of light you can describe on earth. I didn't actually see a person in this light, and yet it has a special identity, it definitely does. It is a light of perfect understanding and perfect love.
>
> The thought came to my mind, 'Lovest thou me?' This was not exactly in the form of a question, but I guess the connotation of what the light said was, 'If you do love me, go back and complete what you began in your life.' And all during this time, I felt as though I were surrounded by an overwhelming love and compassion.[63]

Myths and images of the afterlife, then, remain varied. Our next question is who really is served by the afterlife, God or the human soul?

Chapter 5

God or Garden of Delights? Is Heaven Theocentric or Anthropocentric?

Nirvana, Pure Lands, and All the Heavens Above

What kind of heaven would you want? One of continuous rapture in the worship of God, together with mystical union with God, source of all love, joy, and peace? Or a heaven of unending pure pleasure of the sort we humans delight in here below: fabulous palaces and gardens, transcendent music, wonderful games, dances, friendships, even sensual love?

Both styles are well represented in the world's spiritual traditions. Take for example Buddhism. Here two options – and a mediating third – are laid out fair and square.

The Buddhist heavens of the gods or devas (the word reminds us that the Buddhist gods are mainly carried over from Hinduism) are rewards for good karma, essentially for following the Four Noble Truths. (Life is full of suffering, suffering is caused by attachments, there can be an end to suffering [by ending attachments], the way to end it is living according to the Eightfold Path: right view, right intentions, right speech, right conduct, right livelihood, right effort, right mindfulness, right concentration or meditation.)

The good karma engendered by right living does not lead to eternal life in heaven, much less to release from the wheel of birth and death altogether. But good karma does entitle one to rebirth as a god or deva for a lifetime that can last billions of years in one of the higher heavens, until the stream of positive energy finally runs out, and one is perforce reborn on earth. Even then, as a legacy of that good karma, the birth may be to good family, and in circumstances that will make further spiritual advance easy, perhaps even full Buddhic enlightenment in a few more lifetimes.

We have already noted in connection with *The Tibetan Book of the Dead* that Buddhist reincarnation is not just rebirth in another human life, but depending on one's karma can be in any of six lokas or possible realms of reincarnation: the heaven of the gods, the human realm, the place of the asuras or titans, the animal plane, as one of the hungry ghosts, or the hells.

Popular Buddhist preachers, like ordinary preachers in virtually all religions, have not been hesitant to reinforce their strictures with evocations of hell-fire. The great Japanese Zen teacher Hakuin (1685–1768), raised in Nichiren Buddhism, recounts how as a young child, on hearing a sermon of that sect expound on the agonies of hell, he ran terrified out of the temple, shaking violently. On another occasion, when his mother made his bath a little too hot, he again became fearful of the infernal fires and had to be calmed down.

The Buddhist hells were fearsome places, to be sure. They are several, some of fire and some of ice. In all cases they may be said to represent the inner state of a person who has isolated herself or himself from others, and above all from the great Buddhist virtue of compassion or 'feeling with,' through anger and abusiveness (fire), or through unfeeling coldness (ice). The hell-being was, on earth, the sort of individual who drives away those who try to befriend him, and no less rebuffs those who seek help from her. But, as with all hatred, the ultimate upshot is destructive self-hatred, and fiery or icy self-hatred is the real self-inflicted punishment of hell.

The worst hell, Avichi, said to be fate of one who kills his parents or an enlightened being, is characterized by the excruciation of absolute solitude, and to last as long as it would take a bird to empty a barrel of sesame seeds if it carried away only one in a century. Yet it will, like all Buddhist heavens and hells governed by karma, finally come to an end, for one's karmic debts however great can never be unlimited. But while the worst sinners – or, more accurately, self-destructive persons – may send themselves to the hells, the other lokas are significant self-imposed fates as well.

The realm of the hungry ghosts, beings with huge bellies and tiny mouths, suits those who are continually desiring, including those individuals who 'have it all' yet seem always to want more. The animal plane – the only one of the lokas other than the human ordinarily visible to human sight – is the natural end of a life marked by mere stupidity and the indulgence of the sensual appetites; preachers were known, for example, to display a pig with alleged human features, claiming the animal had been a man whose gluttony led to this unpleasant rebirth. Persons whose lives were marked by anger and violence were likely candidates for the plane of the asuras, whose usual state was fighting one another. As we will see in a moment, in Japanese literature that condition was the destiny of innumerable great samurai warriors.

First, however, we may consider the high, transhuman plane remaining. The heavens of the gods (devas), much in contrast to the lower states, are places of ceaseless delight. Imagine a life of floating indolently on perfumed seas, as hours become days, days become years, and years centuries, all the while listening to the most glorious music as your mind drifts lazily from one engaging fantasy to another, or you talk delightedly with your most beloved friends. You have become a deva, or god. Life is good, and you hardly take the trouble to remember that eventually even this will come to an end.

The heavens, according to most lists, consist of 26 planes above the human loka, presided over by Brahma, the Hindu creator-god. These in turn are divided into three sets: the six realms of the kama-loka, or world of desire; the sixteen of the rupa-loka, or world of highly refined forms; and the four of the arupa-loka, or formless world.

The kama-loka offers tangible paradises of blissful sights and sounds, smells and tastes, generated by relatively pure forms of desire, such as yearning for sociability and beauty. Far from being realms governed by the grosser sensuous desires, such as those of the asuras, animals, hungry ghosts, or hell-beings, they can instead fundamentally be thought of as projections of relatively innocent visions and fantasies. The residue of dreams over countless ages have given the heaven-dweller celestial choir-worlds like those of the *gandhabbas*, or divine musicians; fairylands of devas who dwell in castles in the air; or the enchanted realms of gods who take pleasure in making or transforming worlds according to their pleasure. A few other notes are struck: the lowest heaven-plane above the humans is home not only to the divine musicians, but also to *yakkhas*, spirits like the goblins, trolls, and elves of western lore.

The fourth plane up, the Tushita heaven, is the dwelling-place of the bodhisattva Maitrya, the next Buddha, until the time comes round for his birth in this world. The sixth, the highest of the kama-loka, said to be the realm of devas creating pleasures for one another, paradoxically is also the residence of Mara, tempter of the Buddha on the eve of his enlightenment and now seducer of all beings beneath him by his deceptions. His name is related to words for death, yet he is also said to be a Vedic god of love – perhaps suggesting the mysterious eternal relationship of sex and death, the reproductive urge being that which brings into the world beings born but to die.

Above the kama-loka, the rupa-loka's realms are accessible only to those who have realized some experience in high meditative states called jhanas. These are attained through the practice of samatha, a form of meditation that aims not at Nirvana or Buddhahood, but at subtle peaceful conditions of mind. They are inaugurated through 'one-pointed' concentration, that is, focus on a single object until the mind is stilled. These objects traditionally are forty in number, and range from innocuous discs of different colors to lurid visions of decaying corpses. Dwellers in the rupa-loka are free of any kind of desire, even the highest and most aesthetic, but still are governed by form; they are said to be made of light, and to be occupied with purely mental pleasures.

Finally, the four arupa-loka levels reflect jhanas or meditations that have transcended form altogether; their four realms reflect the crux of such meditation: infinite space, infinite consciousness, nothingness, neither perception nor non-perception.

Such disembodied heavens, making their unimaginable paradises out of the substance of inner states attained only in the profoundest kinds of meditation, may seem so rarefied as to be virtually indistinguishable from Nirvana. Yet, like all Buddhist heavens, they are no more than the reward of good karma, generated by good thoughts, words, and deeds, enhanced by high meditation, and last only until that positive merit is exhausted. They are *still* conditioned reality, not to be confused with Nirvana, unconditioned reality, or even the Pure Lands of the Buddhas which are like ante-chambers to Nirvana. In fact, ordinarily one cannot realize Nirvana in the heavens, for the simple reason that pleasure, or mystical absorption, is therein so intense that the mind is virtually drugged, unable to break out of heaven's blissful intoxication long enough to make those final meditations of analysis (vipassana) that lead to true Enlightenment and Nirvana.

For that reason, after lives in any other loka, from the heavens to the hells, one is ultimately reborn as a human being. Only here, in our world of good and evil, pleasure and pain, day and night, and enough intelligence to make good decisions if one truly wishes to do so, can one vow to become a Buddha and do so, leaping off the wheel of death and rebirth represented by the six lokas altogether and enter Nirvana.

Many Buddhist teachers and preachers interpret the six lokas in metaphorical ways. Despite Hakuin's childhood experience, Nichiren instructors are likely to emphasize they are not just after death, but here and now. In the course of a single hour, you may know a few moments when you feel in absolute hell, a few given over to fantasies drawn out of the gross appetites, a few when you just feel stupid and sensual like an animal, certain moments of raw anger when you could 'just kill' that person, a few seconds or minutes of blissful delight, perhaps even a few ticks of the clock when you are just a human being. If you are fortunate, that hour may also measure a few steps up the road to Nirvanic enlightenment and getting off the wheel altogether. The point is not to worry about life after death, but about what loka you are in here and now. Zen teachers would probably say the whole idea of the afterlife, or fussing about one's reincarnation, is an attachment pulling one away from what is truly important: just being here now, a realized Buddha in the present moment.

Finally, consider as an example one of the No plays of Japan, those dramas of enigmatic simplicity and psychological profundity, hinting at mysterious depths of meaning in human life almost beyond the limits of ordinary thought. 'Tsunemasa,' is a No play by Zeami Motokiyo (1363–1443), the greatest writer of the genre. Tsunemasa, a samurai killed in battle, is now like most of his lot in the realm of the asuras. However, this warrior, unlike most, is not a fighter at heart; his true love is music, his instrument the lute. The emperor ordered a temple being built honoring this fallen hero; at its dedication a few notes were ceremonially plucked on the strings of Tsunemasa's own beloved lute.

Far away in the dreadful land of the asuras, across the gulfs separating worlds, the unhappy warrior heard those familiar sounds and was drawn back, returning as a specter in gorgeous court dress. He had a few moments respite from his punishment as he danced to the melody of his own instrument. But then he cries out that the dreadful passions of asuraland are rising in him, and he must return till his karma is expiated. The chorus sings the tragedy of his fate. So also the fate of all caught up on the turning wheel of life, birth after birth, death after death, until the alternative of liberation fully arises.

Again, all these states, however subtle, are on the wheel of death and rebirth. Even an entity so refined as to be able to spend a lifetime of billions of years enjoying a state of neither perception nor non-perception retains just enough of conditioned reality finally to be brought back to human birth. As the eminent western Buddhist Lama Govinda said of the devic heavens generally:

Devas [i.e. those in the realm of the gods] lead a carefree life, dedicated to aesthetic pleasures ... On account of this one-sided dedication to their own pleasures, they forget the true nature of life, the limitations of their existence, the sufferings of other beings as well as their own transiency . . . They live, so to say, on the accumulated capital of past good deeds without adding any new values. They are gifted with beauty, longevity and freedom from pain, but just this lack of suffering of obstacles and exertion, deprives the harmony of their existence of all creative impulses, all spiritual activity and the urge for deeper knowledge. Thus finally they sink again into lower states of existence.[64]

Then, however, the pilgrim might enter Nirvana itself by setting aside samatha meditation (said to be essentially a training practice) and take up instead vipassana, the meditation of analysis, involving only three hard-hitting topics: the unsatisfactoriness of all conditioned reality, its impermanence, and the unreality of any real ego. Truly knowing these three truths through and through, one slips into Nirvana, the flame of attachment and desire blown out.

It should not be thought, as it often is by non-Buddhists, that Nirvana is a merely negative, even deathlike, state. Quite the opposite, it is the total absence of all that causes those 'little deaths' by which our lives are wracked: insatiable desire, anxiety, the constant change and decay that leads to the frustration of dreams and the choking of hope. Nirvana is said in the Dhammapada (a very early Buddhist text) to be indeed the highest happiness, but happiness unconditioned, uncaused by any impermanent thing. It is not a place, but a state of mind (Mahayanists would say one can have it here and now, amid everyday life), a consciousness radiant with inner stillness and peace. It is described as coolness, without feature, without end yet timeless, suffused with a kind of golden luminosity.

Finally, it remains to mention again the Pure Land of Mahayana Buddhism. It is like a middle ground between the devic heavens and Nirvana, even perhaps the best of both. The Pure Land is a visible, tangible realm, containing the palaces of bodhisattvas together with the flowers and jewels of paradise. Yet it is also unconditioned and as it were merging into Nirvana, because it is the product not of good karma but of the infinite meditative bliss and power of a cosmic buddha.

The First Christian Heavens

Christian images of heaven have long lived in tension between several ideals: on one hand, the theocentric view of heaven as a state where only adoration of God obtains and all else falls away; on the other, the picture, supported by scripture and much folklore, of heaven fledged out as a golden city or as lush gardens, as it were an eternal Eden above. Indeed, a secondary tension lies between those 'rural' and 'urban' prospects: Is paradise green pastures where sheep may safely graze, or the heavenly Jerusalem with its jeweled gates and golden streets? The paradise of open land was well described by John Bunyan in his seventeenth-century Puritan classic, *Pilgrim's Progress*. On his way to Mt. Zion, Christian, the Pilgrim, stayed overnight at the Palace Beautiful, of which its porter said, 'This house was built by the Lord of the hill . . . for the relief and security of pilgrims.' The next morning, looking south from the top of the house, 'at a great distance, he saw a most pleasant mountainous country, beautified with woods, vine-yards, fruits of all sorts, flowers also with springs and fountains, very delectable to behold (Isa. 32:16, 17). Then he asked the name of the country. They [the blessed family of the Palace Beautiful] said it was Immanuel's Land.' But when he came there, his hosts went on, 'thou mayest see to the gate of the Celestial City, as the shepherds that live there will make appear.'[65]

Finally, is heaven only an individual experience for each inhabitant thereof, or a community with ranks and relationships like those of earth, though of course without earth's imperfections? Do new-comers meet and recognize as such their parents, spouses, and children, or would a condition of being 'neither married nor given in marriage' exclude all merely human affection, and one gazes on God alone?

These were knotty problems, and understandably the Christian church has wavered among them. Characteristically, highly prestigious theologians, like Thomas Aquinas and the great Protestant reformers, favored a strictly theocentric icon of the place where God is seen face to face, only for it to crumble around the edges, particularly on the plane of popular religion, as ordinary believers respond with dissatis-faction to what sounded like being in church for all eternity. Surely, if heaven is the perfect place, it ought to allow for innocent dancing, friendship, even human love, as well. Ultimately, of course, behind this conundrum lies the metaphysical problem – and today apparently it is a scientific physics problem as well – of time over against eternity, or whatever is before or outside the space-time continuum. Appropriately, then, we may begin examining Christian thought about heaven with St. Augustine, who as so often sowed the seeds of both sides of later theological arguments, and who famously said of time, 'When no one asks me, I know what time is; when someone asks me to explain it, I do not know' (Confessions, Bk 11).

But the bishop of Hippo was nonetheless convinced, like modern cosmologists, that time exists only within the created universe, and God is outside, in an eternal now. Therefore if the saints worship him unceasingly for all eternity, those endless hymns never get boring, since the singing all takes place in one magnificent moment, and naught else is before, after, or beside the timeless moment. So it was that in *The City of God*, much influenced by Neoplatonism with its similar view of the One as alone and beyond space and time, Augustine's heaven was all consumed by the joy of 'seeing God': 'There we shall rest and see, see and love, love and praise. This is what shall be in the end without end.' And again, 'He [God] shall be the end of our desires who shall be seen without end, loved without cloy, praised without wariness.' No need there is for any other activity, and no occasion of it.[66]

Later in life Augustine softened his position to allow the deceased in heaven physical bodies – even eating and drinking, though just for pleasure, not necessary nourishment – and meeting friends and loved ones, although he insisted that since all were equal there, this did not entail hierarchical or familial relationships. Often early Christian portraits of heaven, including Augustine's, were partially inspired by classical writers on the Golden Age and the afterlife, like those attributed to Hesiod, Plato, Virgil, or Cicero, in which there was frolicsome play and many meetings, though also some purposive activity, as in the choosing of vehicles for future lifetimes in Er's vision – although Christians did not usually allow for reincarnation.

The same veering between the theocentric and anthropocentric heaven can be found in medieval Christian authorities. A woman visionary called Gerardesca (1210–1269) combined the two, as well as rural and urban images, as she described a series of castles set amid beautiful hills; the Holy Trinity dwelt in a central city, the Heavenly Jerusalem, together with the Blessed Virgin, choirs of angels, and the holiest saints; other saints of various degrees inhabited the farther strongholds; the lush surrounding fields were empty because in this feudal paradise there were no peasants, only lords.[67] We may recall our earlier account of Mechthild of Magdeburg vision of hierarchical choirs of saints and angels, apparently all within a vast palace of many stories, including the 'secret chamber' in the highest where the saintliest of virgins could meet alone with Christ.

The great St. Thomas Aquinas, following the dictates of his powerful logic, taught that heaven, being perfect, can allow for no activity, only contemplation of the Beatific Vision, God face to face. While no finite soul can know the infinite God wholly, the exploration of those divine depths through contemplation takes eternity, and suffices for it. Dante transferred this tremendous perception into verse, presenting, as tradition required, the ranked choirs of angels and assemblies of saints. But he found no ambition among them to move higher, for their place was God's will, and *e 'n la sua volontade è nostra pace* – 'In his will is our peace.'[68]

But perhaps not enough for all, for soon enough allowances had to be made. Giles of Rome (1247–1316), though a student of Aquinas, and the famous Franciscan theologian St. Bonaventure (1221–1274), both insisted that the saints in heaven must also comprise a perfect society, and this can only include friendship, though general among all and not exclusive, together with normal human activities in ideal form.[69]

Yet the age of the troubadours and fresh stirrings of romantic love could not forbid lover and beloved, with all that entailed, from heaven either. Many poets sought to reconcile, or sometimes choose between, the face of God and that of the earthly ideal. The most successful such venture was no doubt Dante's *Vita Nuova*, in which the beloved Beatrice, who in the *Divine Comedy* was to guide her admirer up the ladders of heaven, has here in this earlier verse revealed herself even in earthly life to be a lens radiating divine glory, what Charles Williams called the Beatrician vision, which of itself can save as it were by proxy for God. In *Vita Nuova* the poet sang, 'Her least salutation bestows salvation on this favored one, and humbles him till he forgets all wrong.' Should the point be missed, the Florentine went on to say, 'This too has God Almighty graced her with: whoever speaks with her shall speak with Him.'[70]

Nor was this sacred beauty lost by her early death, at age 24. After great grief, Dante was in the end able to see the divine grace radiated through her now as it were universalized, available to recipient souls everywhere:

> This is because the pleasure of her beauty,
> having removed itself from mortal sight,
> was transformed into beauty of the soul
> spreading throughout the heavens . . .[71]

In time, in the *Divine Comedy*, she would become his intercessor in the Inferno, his saving love in Purgatory, his guide in Paradise.

In a preface to Shakespeare's sonnets, the poet W. H. Auden, refer-ring to Dante and Beatrice as well as to the English bard's mysterious 'fair youth' and 'dark lady' of the sonnets, asserted that occasionally a rare and divinely inspired vision can imbue a person in the eyes of another with shining light, to which one can feel drawn and even united; he considered Shakespeare saw this mysterious glory in the fetching unknown persons to whom these sonnets are addressed.[72]

So it is that in the art and letters of Renaissance humanists the anthropocentric heaven breaks through in full spate, even flooding earth and leaving behind its reflective pools. As for heaven, in a paint-ing like Fra Angelico's *Last Judgment* (c. 1431) the blessed, once they hear the favorable decree, are shown rejoicing with dance steps, meet-ing and greeting, pairing off. In this great work, one even perceives the remarkable image of a female angel chastely yet firmly embracing a presumably heretofore celibate monk. Celso Maffei (1425–1508), though himself also monastic, described in some detail the embraces and kisses that will occur in heaven between the saints and Christ himself.[73] Much more could be cited as Renaissance masters scarcely bothered to conceal their lively delight in the sensual world of pagan antiquity, and strove to reconcile it with Christianity by whatever means necessary. How else to explain the Virgin Marys who are at once Mother of God and quite beautiful women, divinely human like Dante's Beatrice, or the charmingly naked Christ Childs – all what Dante called 'the glorious and holy flesh' – and these heaven on earth figures set against lush landscapes?

Nietzsche once suggested that art enables us to bear reality (see e.g., *The Birth of Tragedy*, section 3), meaning presumably that brush and scalpel put the overwhelming weight of eternity – or, if one prefer, Nietzschean eternal recurrence – within the human form, behind the human face, or above the grandeur of nature, so that we can live with it day by day, yet never without reminder of what will always be beyond the ultimate reach of change and decay. A face painted by Raphael, or the flawless youth immortalized in Michelangelo's *David*, will itself wither and die, but the radiant beauty in the painting, like the marble form, will be forever filled with the glory of God. Even after her early death, Beatrice was Dante's guide in heaven. The art of the Renaissance not only rediscovered the everyday, but also intro-duced everyday life into heaven, though there of course in the form of those timeless moments of everyday joy when past and future are forgotten: those Fra Angelico dancers will never weary, those lovers will never quarrel.

Protestant Heavens

The Protestant Reformation represented a powerful swing back to the theocentric heaven, above all for the two principal reformers, Martin Luther and John Calvin. Indeed, they both wanted to put God at the absolute center of everything: God's will and sovereign grace, God's word in the Bible, God's priority in all human life. In his Table Talks, Luther emphasized that heaven would be without change, without eating and drinking or anything to do in the ordinary sense: 'But I think we will have enough to do with God.'[74] The German reformer insisted that at death souls would go directly to the Last Day, without delay in Purgatory or anywhere else, so as immediately to join his or her resurrected body and face final judgment. But the Lutheran church itself was to revert to the medieval view of souls lingering in an immaterial body, in a sort of temporary afterlife, in the intervening time between expiration and resurrection.

Even for the great reformer, though, heaven could require softening and humanizing for the sake of weaker brethren, or perhaps for the sake of powerful symbolic images. When his beloved daughter Magdalene talked of heaven as a place where she could get 'lots of apples, pears, sugar, plums, and so on,' her father only encouraged her, and he told his son Hans that heaven would be 'a pretty, beautiful and delightful garden where there are many children wearing little golden coats. They pick up fine apples, pears, cherries, and yellow and blue plums under the trees. They sing, jump, and are merry. They also have nice ponies.'[75]

John Calvin no less emphasized the theocentric centrality of the deity and his worship in heaven, even insisting that the saints would not speak to each other, only to God. Yet even the two principal reformers and their leading followers were not always consistent, not only when speaking to children, but also in their substantive theological work. Both, following scripture, affirmed that the eschaton would bring a new, perfected earth, complete with perfect and eternal plants and animals.

The animals, and even wood and stone, may well share in the glorious resurrection at the end, conceded Calvin, for did not the apostle Paul declare that 'the creation waits with eager longing for the revealing of the sons of God . . . because the creation itself will be set free from its bondage to decay and obtain the glorious liberty of the children of God' (Rom. 8:19–21)? Yet the Geneva reformer was reticent concerning details of the resurrected life, or life in heaven, saying only that 'the end of the resurrection is eternal happiness, of whose excellence scarcely the minutest part can be described by all that human tongues can say. For though we are truly told that the kingdom of God will be full of light, and gladness, and felicity, and glory, yet the things meant by these words remain most remote from sense, and as it were involved in enigma, until the day arrive on which he will manifest his glory to us face to face.'[76]

The new earth, promised in prophecy, will also then be manifested. Yet the resurrected elect would not abide there, since heaven was their home and the glory of God their work, though they could 'contemplate' it to the divine glory, and (according to Luther) could visit our now-perfected world on excursions. Luther also once mentioned the prospect of greeting his father in heaven and talking with him; the next generation of reformers, including such figures as Melanchthon and Mathesius, felt able to speculate more freely on meeting friends and loved ones on the other side, though stressing that neither families nor states would be reconstituted there since, being of their time and place, they could think of such units only in terms of authority – father over wife and children, prince over people – and in heaven all were absolutely equal. Yet, for many Protestants, the stark two-way choice confronting them in 'death, and after that the judgment,' that was all left them following the death of Purgatory, seemed inadequate to allow for fine gradations of terror and bliss to fit the fluctuations of virtue observed by ordinary people in the human world around them and, if they were honest, in themselves. Something more seemed needed.

A new, more humane and educational, idea of the afterlife emerged in some Protestant circles after the eighteenth century. The new picture was strongly tinctured by the writings of Emanuel Swedenborg (1688–1772). No doubt reflecting new values in European society – the rise of the nuclear family, Rousseau-like ideas of 'natural' childhood and education, even the emergence of democratic ideals – the visions of the Swedish sage implicitly rejected a forensic, individual-judgment notion in favor of what might be called a 'therapeutic' view of the Afterlife.

The son of a Swedish Lutheran bishop, Swedenborg was drawn to science as a young man, making significant contributions to metallurgy and mining engineering (he served on the Swedish Board of Mines) as well as other fields. But in midlife his searching intellect turned to philosophical and spiritual concerns as well. He wrote books such as *The Economy of the Animal Kingdom* (1740–1741) arguing that the soul ('animal' in the title is the Latin *anima*, soul), though non-material, represents the life-energy moving all things. Then, in 1744–1745, the

Swedish sage passed through a sort of initiation into a new level of perception and life. He believed he encountered God himself in direct experience, and conversed with the divine Lord as one to another. The Almighty told the initiate seer that he would be shown the realm of spirits, including heaven and hell, and should write about them.

This he did, in voluminous tomes documenting a remarkable series of visionary experiences, in which he believed he traveled personally to heaven and hell. The Swede's accounts of the two destinations are clearly the products, based on careful empirical observation, of a systematic scientific mind. In brief, he saw both as states, not places, to which spirits are drawn by their own nature, forming communities of souls congenial in temperament under the guidance of angels, who are themselves simply departed humans risen to the higher levels of heaven, the Celestial. In Swedenborg's heaven like-minded are drawn together, children are nurtured, and marriages of love take place between congenial spirits. Although the presence of God is everywhere, and is the hidden force governing the contours of heavenly society, Swedenborg's heaven is anthropocentric in the sense that human hearts do not occupy themselves with the direct and continual worship of God. Church services are not required; the Lord is content to be praised through the blessed souls' happy activities and their love for each other; he desires no further honor.

The nature of one's afterlife depends on the character of the person. Each gradually ascends or descends to heavenly or hellish townships according to his or her bent, kind or cruel.[77] It is the presence of God which makes a state heaven and hell. The highest angels are closest in spirit to the divine glory; their heaven is made up of innumerable societies of souls joyous and deeply loving in their own way, corresponding to the many different ways of happiness on earth. He visited a city of Athenian philosophers; one envisions countless others perhaps of artists, engineers, dancers, and all the innocent diversity of humankind's inner dispositions. Each of these park-like cities would be filled with wonderful conversation, delightful acts of mutual kindness, and of course literally endless creativity. Heaven is also the site of conjugal meetings, and seldom echoes with the joyous festivity of weddings; celestial marriages are of an ideal spiritual sort very seldom seen on earth.

Hell, on the other hand, is peopled by those who turn their backs on God. 'The Lord does not cast anyone into hell: spirits cast themselves in ... For all the people who are in the hells are absorbed in evils and consequent falsities because of their love for themselves and the world.'[78] No one is born for hell; that is a choice one makes. When spirits first arrive in the spirit world, they want nothing more than to go to heaven. For this reason they are taken to the outer perimeters of paradise. But 'If they are devoted to love for themselves and the world, then the moment they reach the first border of that heaven they begin to feel pain and to be so tormented within that they feel as though they were in hell rather than in heaven. So they themselves dive down head-long and are not at rest until they are with their own kind in the hells.'[79] Whether any of these hell-beings could leave hell for heaven is perhaps an unanswered question, since the sage was repeatedly told by them they would a thousand times rather live down below than anywhere else. The terrain which looked so barren to angels, and visages appearing so ugly to innocence, was to eyes moved mainly by lust or cruelty appealing.

Immediately after death, most souls then enter a 'Spiritual World,' where they remain from a few days up to as long as thirty years, determining, sometimes by trial and error, where their place lies in this strange, light-filled new environment. The good news is that all these states, being self-imposed, are not permanent. Spirits can advance from lower to higher planes of heaven as they grow in wisdom and love. In this respect it is clear that the eighteenth-century master's vision has a modern ring: it represents the 'triumph of the therapeutic' and of education over forensic and punitive concepts of the afterlife still prevalent in many quarters.

Although the Swedenborgian church, properly called the Church of the New Jerusalem, has remained very small, the Swede's influence went far beyond church walls. Emerson and New England Transcendentalism, together with movements like Spiritualism, Theosophy, and New Thought, all show imprints of Swedenborgian thought. In particular, the picture of heaven in novels like those of Elizabeth Stuart Phelps, presented in our first chapter, could hardly be imagined without Age of Enlightenment mystic's earlier explorations.

The Hidden Paradise

Finally, let us consider the notion of paradises on this earth, but inhabited by immortals or the departed. We have already mentioned the Taoist western paradise and the island eastern one, home to immortals but occasionally glimpsed by others, and the mysterious western supernatural realms of Celtic lore, or the classical Isles of the Blessed.

A comparable vision was attributed to the mythical Yellow Emperor, the first Chinese ruler who presided over a primordial golden age. The writings of the Taoist Liezi (fl. fourth century B.C.E.) tell us that, after doing certain spiritual exercises, the ancient sovereign fell asleep in the daytime, and dreamed he was conveyed to a paradise realm tens of thousands of miles away. This Taoist utopia was without head or ruler; but simply 'went on of itself,' for 'its people were without desires or craving; they simply followed their natural instincts.' Merely by perfectly conforming to the essence of nature they developed what would seem to be supernatural powers: they could walk through the air, and see through clouds and mist, and even more important were unattached either to life or death. Returning, the primal monarch learned the great lessons that the Tao is not to be sought through the senses, and true rulership lies in not attempting to regulate the lives of others, but freeing them to discover their own inner nature and then live by it.[80]

Undoubtedly among the most potent of all such earthly paradises is Shambhala, the mythical kingdom beyond the Himalayas credenced in many parts of the East as well as by some western occultists. Indeed, it was probably one inspiration for the famous novel by James Hilton, *Lost Horizon*, about the chance discovery of Shangri-La, a hidden valley west of China far from the tumult of a world lurching toward war; the tale also became a classic film in 1937.[81]

Myths of Shambhala, best known in Tibet, speak of it as an abode of enlightened beings; some say of bodhisattvas who reincarnate in the world as needed. The fabulous land is ruled over by a series of righteous kings, each of whom reigns about a hundred years. It is said the present age of the universe will conclude during the reign of the twenty-fifth. Then an evil tyrant will conquer the rest of the earth, but the last king, called Rudrachakrin, will go forth to defeat him by force of spiritual power. That marvelous event will be followed by a millennium of peace and the spread of the true dharma everywhere. Some scholars have set the exact date of Rudrachakrin's victory at 2354 C.E. by the western calendar.

But the nature and location of Shambhala are not entirely clear. Traditional geographers have tried to locate possible sites among the remote mountains, deserts, and oases of central Asia, or (if historically minded) have speculated that the idea was sparked by one of the isolated Buddhist kingdoms once found beyond those forbidding and almost endless ranges. Guidebooks were published for the journey to Shambhala, although often the venture was presented in terms more suggestive of a spiritual initiation than a secular exploration. Thus the sixteenth century Rinpungpa, after lengthy accounts of fearsome obstacles and temptations on the way, ends his wonderfully poetic Shambhala manual in this way:

> After crossing the mountains, you will have to go through one last forest filled with snakes and wild animals, but if you show friendliness and compassion to whatever creatures you meet, you will have no trouble. Although you feel exhausted and sick from the rigors of the journey, hold onto your aim and continue to dedicate your efforts to the benefit of all beings.
>
> Then you will see, at last, the cities of Shambhala, gleaming among ranges of snow mountains like stars on the waves of the Ocean of Milk. Flowers of light . . . will remove all ignorance from your mind and leave you happy and refreshed, completely recovered from the hardships of your journey. Now you can drink and rest and enjoy the fruits of all your efforts . . .[82]

Clearly Shambhala is no ordinary journey or place. Certain authorities have averred that, like the western Grail Castle at Carbonek, it is sometimes seen and sometimes not; one traveler may espy its gleaming towers, another looking the same way see naught but desolation and fog. Others are of the opinion the enlightened kingdom is entirely on another plane, to be found inwardly rather than in some outer geographical location. This brings it into the world of the hidden paradises of mystics and visionaries.

George Fox (1624–1691), founder of the Quakers, wrote in his *Journal* (pub. 1694): 'Now was I come up in spirit through the flaming sword into the paradise of God. All things were new, and all the creation gave another smell unto me than before, beyond what words can utter.'[83] Fox's contemporary, the Anglican clergyman and metaphysical poet Thomas Traherne (1636–1674) in his remarkable work *Centuries of Meditations* describes a childhood in which 'I saw all in the peace of Eden . . . all time was Eternity . . . The corn was orient and immortal wheat . . . the dust and stones of the street were as precious as gold . . . The green trees . . . transported and ravished me . . . almost mad with ecstasy, they were such strange and wonderful things . . . Boys and girls tumbling in the street . . . were moving jewels . . .'[84]

Clearly these seventeenth-century paradises were no locations, but rather ways of seeing: ways of seeing a world which to other eyes would have been not jewels but only dross. But to them the sight – even, for Fox, the smell! – was charged with the poet William Wordsworth's

> . . . sense sublime
> Of something far more deeply interfused,
> Whose dwelling is the light of setting suns,
> And the round ocean . . . and the mind of man;
> A motion and a spirit, that . . .
> . . . rolls through all things.

Some, of course, have perceived somewhat similar visions of the glory within by means of psychedelic drugs. Their use was known to many primal people; indeed the theory has been advanced that such visions on the part of paleolithic shamans were an origin of religion, and that the famous cave paintings were attempts to record those transcendent manifestations.[85] For the Huichol of Mexico, the psychedelic cactus peyote remains close to inner spiritual essence. One Huichol informant said to an anthropologist:

> You people take photographs. You come with us on the pilgrimage and even partake of the peyote. But you never ask 'why' to the peyote. You never ask. Well, I'm going to tell you: peyote is every-thing, it is the crossing of the souls, it is everything that is. Without peyote nothing would exist, but you people never ask why.[86]

People in other cultures have likewise tried the sacred drug. Perhaps the most famous such account is Aldous Huxley's *The Doors of Perception*, describing the experience of taking mescaline, a derivative of peyote. The great novelist and essayist speaks, for example, of looking at an ordinary lawn chair:

> That chair – shall I ever forget it? Where the shadows fell on the canvas upholstery, stripes of a deep but glowing indigo alternated with stripes of an incandescence so intensely bright that is was hard to believe that they could be made of anything but blue fire. For what seemed an immensely long time I gazed without knowing, even without wishing to know, what it was that confronted me . . . a chair which looked like the Last Judgment – or, to be more accurate, by a Last Judgment I recognized as a chair.[87]

Huxley, compiler of the splendid mystical anthology *The Perennial Philosophy*, is certainly not so naive as to confuse psychedelic with true mystical experience. This mescaline experiment was only opening the doors of perception a crack. Yet all these visions – and one could go on to mention poets like William Blake or AE (George Russell) – tell us one thing, that paradise is not just far away, it is also, for those who have eyes to see, right in front us, nearer than hands and feet, perhaps deep within or in the eyes of those for whom Blake wrote when he said: 'If the doors of perception were cleansed every thing would appear to man as it is, infinite.'[88]

For them it was not necessary even to die to go to heaven.

Chapter 6

Ghostly Fear and Love: The Dread of Ancestral Spirits vs. Respect and Honor

Friendly and 'Scary' Spirits

A colorful midsummer festival in Japan is Obon, the annual welcoming back of spirits of the dead. Often held July 13–16, though dates may vary in different locations, it is a time when extended families endeavor to return to their original homes to meet again relatives both of this world and of the next world. Families first visit the cemetery to clean the graves carefully, and set out bowls of water, rice, other food, and flowers as offerings. They then return to the family home to clean and decorate it with flowers and traditional ornaments so the dead will feel welcome there as well.

On the morning of the fourteenth, it is customary for the extended family to gather at their principal house to prepare the tablets inscribed with the names of departed that will be placed at household altars. It is also the custom to visit friends and neighbors at this time who have recently lost a loved one, bringing appropriate gifts. Generally, Buddhist priests will perform services with the chanting of sutras and offering of clouds of incense in homes and temples on behalf of the departed.

Best known of all Obon customs are the traditional Obon dances, usually great circle dances performed outdoors, to welcome the returning spirits and then, at the end of the festival, to see them off. The lively energy of these dances suggests that Obon is fundamentally a happy occasion; ghosts come back to be among us, so long as they are relatives or of our family lineage, do not cause feelings of sadness or dread, but rather rejoicing. Many Obon festivities include carnivals with rides, games, and food. The Obon ends with *toro nagashi*, the floating of lanterns. Illumined paper lanterns are floated down rivers to symbolize the ancestors' return to the world of the dead.

Even then, they may not stay entirely away. There is also a broader cultus of ancestral spirits, called *mitama*, especially developed in some of the 'new religions' of Japan such as Konkokyo. *Mitama* assist and guide their loved ones in the land of the living. One often hears people remark that the *mitama* are with them, sending encouraging thoughts and helpful concern.

All this is far from the only attitude toward the dead in Japan, however. The island nation is saturated with ghost stories – stories of the restless spirits of samurai warriors such as the No play cited earlier, stories of hauntings, stories of vengeful ancestors and ill-treated maidens. Unwholesome ghosts may be particularly active on New Year's Eve. An American teacher in Japan, Bruce Feiler, tells of a junior high school student of his who asked, as they walked toward a small Shinto shrine on that evening, 'Have you ever seen a Japanese ghost? We might see one tonight. They are *really* scary.' The boy's older brother added, 'All the ghosts dress in white, and they float in green smoke. But they don't have legs, so you can outrun them.'[89]

Perhaps some perspective can be put on these two kinds of spirits of the dead, welcome and scary, by reference to a myth often cited as the origin of Obon. It is said that a disciple of the Buddha, called Mokuren in Japanese (Mulian in Chinese), was sufficiently advanced spiritually that he could look for his mother in the other worlds. He discovered that, because of exceedingly grievous sins in a previous life, she was condemned to the Avici hell, most horrible of all. He went to his master to ask him how she could be released, and was told to do spiritual works of reparation, including presenting gifts to the monks at the end of their summer retreat on the fifteenth day of the seventh month. Accomplishing these worthy deeds, he gained his mother's release, first from Hell to the realm of the Hungry Ghosts, finally to Heaven. Mulian also gained insight into the many sacrifices she had made for him in life, ill-rewarded though she may have been thereafter. Happy for her liberation and grateful for her kindness, he danced for joy – the first Obon dance.[90]

Here we see the theme both of ghosts and of welcome ancestral spirits. For the preta or hungry ghosts are traditionally believed to be present around us: simple offerings such as a plate of soup are put out for them at festivals such as New Year's as acts of compassion, and to keep them out of mischief. Yet, with far greater compassion like that of

Mokuren, it appears a soul can be released from one realm to another, from being 'scary' to being welcomed.

Roses and Beans

Japan is far from the only society in which such a double image of the departed is obtained. Indeed, it could be argued that the area of death, funerals, and attitudes toward the departed is one in which popular religion around the world tends to converge, regardless of major religious tradition. In the 'West' too, graves are honored with visits and flowers, particularly on occasions such as Memorial Day in the United States, and it is common for people to report feeling the benign presence of loved ones with them. Yet at the same time, tales of fearsome ghosts like the example from Kentucky cited earlier are often heard; even if only half-believed, they are a significant part of folklore. Moreover, Halloween, revived from ancient Celtic and Anglo-Saxon sources, has been a popular holiday for which the ostensible occasion is, as on the Japanese New Year's Eve, the return of 'scary' ghosts and spirits from the other side on this one day when the veil between the worlds grows thin.

Comparable distinctions between good and ominous contacts with the spirits of the dead, and two distinct classes of such spirits, could be multiplied. The Romans celebrated two festivals: the Parentalia on 13–21 February, honoring deceased ancestors, and the Lemuria on 9–13 May designed to drive away evil spirits. The Parentalia was festive and gay, a time of happy remembrance when the necropolis or family tombs were visited, cleaned, and the departed given offerings of food and drink, the family joining in these oblations with their own consumption of food in a kind of picnic. Thus the living and dead came together to celebrate their common bonds. Roses, both at this festival and in other offerings at the funerary altar, were especially favored; they were the last item to be set out, and were regarded as a pledge of an eternal springtime of roses in the life beyond the grave.

The lemurs of Lemuria, on the other hand, were unquiet wraiths who had been left unburied, or improperly buried, so could not rest. Such unwelcome guests were driven out in a bizarre midnight ritual, in which the head of the house, barefoot and making a peculiar gesture of putting his thumb to his forehead, would toss away black beans nine times, saying, 'These I cast, with these I redeem me and mine.' The ghosts were believed to invisibly gather up the beans and thereafter follow the worshiper. The ritualist would next touch water and clash bronze, then finally turning to look toward the ghosts and command, 'Depart, old spirits!'[91]

The Dead Live

Often whether a spirit returns as a welcome guest or fearsome ghost depends upon particular circumstances. In Trinidad, for example, douens are the spirits of unbaptized children who are said to wander the island nation at night seeking living children who have also not yet been baptized to carry off. Douens wear large straw hats to hide their faces, but otherwise are completely naked. If this were not enough, they can be detected by their feet, which turn backwards. They make a seductive whooping sound that will draw unwary unchristened children away from their beds and into their world of night.[92]

The douens are probably related to the duende of Belize, as well as of Mexico and other countries of Hispanic America, mischievous sprites who are especially likely to play tricks on children. A somewhat more imposing figure is San Diego Duende, an assistant to Santa Muerte, 'Saint Death,' an unorthodox (in the eyes of the Roman Catholic Church) but popular cult figure in Mexico. She is stunning with her skull-face and queenly robes, and is believed to be very powerful in answering prayers when her favor is won.[93]

Comparable accounts can be given of the fairies, elves, and other 'little people' of European folklore, also especially dangerous to children. Popular belief attributed several derivations to them: as nature spirits 'built in' to such phenomena as trees, rocks, mountains, streams, and waterfalls; as fallen angels who, according to certain legends, were cast out from heaven with Satan but were not bad enough to accompany him all the way to the fires below, but ended up on earth, half-way between heaven and hell; as the gods and their attendants of pre-Christian faith, such as that of Wotan and Thor or of the ancient Celts; or (this is more recent and academic) folk memories of wild, perhaps diminutive peoples who dwelt in Europe before its present races. By far the most prevalent view, though, is that the fairies have a close connection to the dead. Often it is said that they are the souls of pagans dead before the coming of the Gospel, the wisest among them perhaps spirits of the Druids; not evil, yet being unbaptized ineligible for heaven.[94]

In some cases an even closer relationship may be suggested, and the fairies may be not only the dead of bygone heathen times, but good

Christian dead whose invisible city is not far away but near at hand, within hailing distance. W. Y. Evans-Wentz, in his monumental *The Fairy-Faith in Celtic Countries*, opined that:

> There may be, perhaps, an idea, as there certainly is in the Breton Death-Faith, that the spirits of the faithful dead are all round us, and are not rapt away into a *distant* Paradise or Purgatory. This may be of pre-Christian origin, but does not contradict any article of the Christian faith. The warnings, apparitions, and hauntings, the 'calling of the dead' at sea, and other details of Cornish Death-Legends, seem to point to a conception of a 'plane' of the dead, similar to but not necessarily identical with that of the elementals.[95]

It may even be the fairies that carry off the dead. Evans-Wentz likewise tells of an informant who told him that until after her daughter was born, she would rise up on her elbow in bed to listen to the death-coach passing by, and she was sure it was being driven on its macabre mission by the fairies.

> It passed about midnight, and she could hear the rushing, the tramp-ing of the horses, and most beautiful singing, just like fairy music, but she could not understand the words. Once or twice she was brave enough to open the door and look out as the coach passed, but she could never see a thing, though there was the noise and singing.[96]

The dead can also appear among us, according to the lore of numerous cultures, through possession by the living, so that it is really another soul animating a deceased body. There is a famous story of the great Hindu monk-philosopher Shankara (eighth century C.E.). Like all well-trained brahmins, he was much given to debate with others of his class, contests in which Shankara even when very young was usually victorious. On one occasion he was in public dispute with a certain Mandana Misra. The latter's wife, Bharati, herself a learned woman, served as umpire. The upshot was of considerable consequence to her, since the agreement was that whoever lost would have to accept the other's way of life, meaning that if Mandana faltered he would need to become a celibate like Shankara, and she would in effect be without a husband.

Finally, after seventeen days, he did suffer defeat, but then Bharati herself stepped in to take his place and continue the debate with Shankara. She too seemed bested by the incomparably brilliant intellect facing her – until she began to challenge the young academic philosopher on his knowledge of the Kama Shastra, or science of love. This was one area of which he, an ascetic celibate, could claim no knowledge.

Shankara then begged for a reprieve of one month, in which to prepare himself in this esoteric discipline. The time off was generously granted. Setting off disconsolately with his disciples, the young scholar encountered the funeral procession of a king. Immediately the answer came to him. Using the yogic skills at which he was an incomparable adept, Shankara transferred his soul out of his own body and into that of the deceased monarch. So it was that, to the amazement of his retainers, the ruler rose up from the coffin and went into his palace.

There, taking full advantage of the royal harem, the sage quickly mastered the one area of learning at which he had lacked proficiency. Then – some say after a delay as the appeal of the luxurious and sensuous life began to grow on him, and he even wrote a book on erotics – the ascetic returned to his true body, reportedly just in time, as his carnal remains were about to be burnt. But no longer was there any topic of which he was ignorant. The young Vedantin proved himself as much a master in erotics as in any other field. Mandana reluctantly became a monk, and his superfluous wife Bharati made herself a student of Shankara himself.[97]

Spiritual Wonders

More recent accounts of the appearing and possessing dead can be found in the annals of Spiritualism, especially during its mid-nineteenth-century heyday. One such narrative is Henry Steel Olcott's *People from the Other World*, a classic of the genre describing his visit to the home of the dour Eddy brothers near Chittenden, Vermont, in 1874, where remarkable phenomena was reportedly taking place. Here is an episode from the time of the death of Mrs. Eddy, mother of the two brothers, in the previous year, 1873, after a long illness.

> During the whole time she lay in bed, manifestations of the presence of the departed were frequent ... she needed quiet, and they [the brothers], watching secretly, would see their dead sister Miranda's spirit in materialized form, doing the necessary offices for the invalid. They would hear her talking with their mother, and when it was necessary to turn her, the spirit, with the help of other spirits, would do it.

One day, as they sat at dinner, soft strains of music came through the open door, and going outside, they heard sweet airs played at the corner of the house, by an invisible harp and flute, the sound gradually receding and dying away on the air. A week before she breathed her last, her own dead mother, to warn whom the phantom lady came in her unsubstantial coach, appeared in materialized form to them all, bearing a basket of white roses in her hand. She told them that Mrs. Eddy would soon come 'over the river' to her, and she was waiting to welcome her on the farther shore. The old lady wore the same dress as in life – a brown woolen frock, a round calico cape, a check apron, and a cap on her head; her scissors hung as usual at her side, and no detail was lacking to make her identification complete. She left a message for Horatio [one of the brothers] to the effect that many years before, when about starting on a journey, she had hidden a string of gold beads in a snuff-box in the cellar wall; and directed him to find it and give the necklace to his youngest sister to wear for her sake.[98]

Needless to say, the necklace was found. There seems to be no verification of this account save the brothers' own relation, but it is characteristic of innumerable such stories from folklore and Spiritualism; the significance lies in their witness to the popularity of visits from the other world. Other encounters, however, Olcott claimed to have seen first hand. He tells, for example, of a German music-teacher from Hartford named Max Lenzberg, who was at Chittenden with his wife and daughter. He played the flute at a séance, seated in front of the cabinet from which spirit manifestations were emerging. Then there appeared in the door two children, and behind them an old woman. Mrs. Lenzberg recognized them immediately as her own departed little ones, and eagerly asked in German if this were not so.

Immediately there came several loud responsive raps, and the little Lena [a living child], as if drawn from her mother's side by an irresistible power, crept forward and peered at the forms that stood just at the edge of the black shadows of the cabinet. There was moment's silence as she strained her eyes in the gaze, and then she said joyfully: '*Ja! Ihr seid meine kleine schestern! Nicht wahr?*' There came again responsive raps, and the spirit-forms danced and waved their arms as if in glee at the re-union.[99]

It would be amiss not to present another aspect of Spiritualism and its employment of the deceased: its relationship to religious and social radicalism. Contrary to what one might expect from voices of the dead past, its spirits were frequently strong advocates of reform. They were, in 1850s America, passionate for the abolition of slavery, temperance, the rights of women, and in some cases even free love and the abolition of marriage, viewed as essentially the enslavement of women. A periodical called the *Radical Spiritualist* in 1860 advocated 'Spiritualism, Socialism, Anti-Slavery, Non-Resistance, Women's rights, Anti-Oath-taking and Office-holding, Temperance, Vegetarianism, Anti-Tobacco (Tea, Coffee), and every other Reform which requires the practice of a higher life.'[100]

This stance was, first, because – in a period when progressivism and radicalism of all sorts were seething, often incited initially in the fervent passions aroused by abolitionism – Spiritualism, as a highly unorthodox movement, naturally drew those who were unorthodox in other ways as well to it as a spiritual home. Unbound by the iron hand of scripture or tradition, the spirits and their mouthpieces could bring forth things new as well as old, putting the endorsement of the other world on a new world of freedom, equality, democracy, and all other accouterments of the 'higher life.'

Furthermore, many of the mediums were women, at a time when women had virtually no opportunity for comparable spiritual leadership in conventional churches. It is not surprising, then, that they often gave voice to women's perspectives on what was a man's world. Not a few early feminists, such as Susan B. Anthony and Elizabeth Cady Stanton, if not committed Spiritualists, were sympathetic and recognized the importance of the spiritual movement for the women's movement. In the right circumstances, the dead can see farther into the future than the living and prepare the latter for what must come.

Havens for Heroes

Often, ordinary persons may have one kind of afterlife, warriors and heroes another. As we have seen, most ancient Greeks went to the shadowy realm of Hades, but in time heroes could find rest in the Hesperides or the Isles of the Blest; ordinary German people found themselves in the gloom of Hel, while warriors enjoyed eternal warfare and feasting in the splendor of Valhalla. Let us look a little further at the diverse dwelling-places of the departed.

Hades was both the god of the Underworld and the subterranean realm itself, and his was the original Greek land of the dead. Hades, brother of Zeus and other of the Olympian deities, ruled over that dismal place with his consort Persephone – who, as we may recall from the myth of her mother Demeter, was allowed to return to the earth during the growing season, and thus provide life and fertility above as well as reign over death below. Hades was, in a real sense, both death and renewer of life.

Hades, accessible through certain caverns, was separated from the land of the living by the River Styx, over which one could be conveyed by Hermes in his capacity as psychopomp or guide of souls, or later by the ferryman Charon. In the *Iliad* and *Odyssey*, Hades was apparently the destiny of all non-divine souls who had received proper burial; we recall that Odysseus met there even such heroes as Achilles and Patrokles. (Those who were not given appropriate funeral rites were in even more pathetic state; Odysseus was once visited by the shade of his friend Elpenor, left uninterred on Crete, who had to wonder unable to rest between the living and the dead until the great navigator was able to offer him correct obsequies.)

As time went on, it appears that the dark world of Hades was not considered adequate for all equally. As early as Hesiod, references begin to occur to the Isles of the Blest, or Elysium, to which heroes, undying, are marvelously transported.

> And when Death's veil had covered them over
> Zeus granted them a life apart from other men,
> Settling them at the ends of the Earth.
> And there they live, free from all care,
> In the Isles of the Blest, by Ocean's deep stream,
> Blessed heroes for whom the life-giving Earth
> Bears sweet fruit ripening three times a year.[101]

It will be noted that this wonderful place was not the reward or a favorable moral judgment, nor was it home for all virtuous deceased, but was reserved only for those heroes whom the gods particularly chose to favor. By the sixth to fifth centuries B.C.E., however, Elysium seems to have become more democratic.

The eloquent poet Pindar (c. 518–438 B.C.E.) wrote thus of the blessed:

> But with nights equal forever,
> with sun equal in their days, the good men

have life without labor, disquieting not the earth in strength
   of hand . . .
Beside the great gods
they who had joy in keeping faith lead a life without tears . . .
   there
winds sweep from the Ocean
across the Island of the Blessed. Gold flowers flame
on land in the glory of trees . . .
whence they bind bracelets on their arms and go chapleted . . .[102]

To be sure, Pindar makes clear that the judgment of Hades extends to
the face of the earth, and those not among the blessed 'sustain unface-
able evil.' It is thought that the happy afterlife of the Greeks emerged
partly under the influence of Egypt, whose dead enjoyed a comfortable
and pleasing eternity, and partly due to the increasing influence of
mystery religions with their promise of a blessed afterlife to initiates.
In Plato, as we have seen, and in several other mystic philosophers,
the pleasant fields of the afterlife were only a waystation between one
incarnation and the next.

   Mention may especially be made of the Latin poet Tibullus (c. 54–19
B.C.E.), for whom the innocent Golden Age was not only in the mythic
past, but lived on in the contemporary Elysian Fields of the blessed
dead. For this poet of imperial Rome, though, Elysium was a place for
those who died of love, not war, which he hated. Aboard his Isles of
the Blest, male and female couples, generally naked, spent their time
dancing, playing, bathing and swimming, or making love amid the
delights of singing birds and scented flowers:

My spirit, though, as I have always welcomed tender love,
Venus herself will lead to the Elysian fields.
There songs and dances flourish, and flitting everywhere
sweetly sing the birds their slender-throated tune.
Untilled the land bears cassia and over whole acres
heavy-scented roses bloom from the rich loam.
Young men and tender girls make sport, lined up together,
continually engaging in the battle of Love.
There are all those whom Death raped while they were lovers
and they wear the myrtle in token on their hair.[103]

In this sacred place, free love was no sin. Later moralists, particularly Christian, could not entirely agree, yet chastened versions of pagan gardens of earthly delights covertly made their way into some models of the Christian heaven in its anthropocentric form.

By the time of Virgil's Aeneid, Elysium is but one department of the other world, a place like the Isles of the Blest, but underground with its own sun and stars, where past heroes are rewarded and future heroes await auspicious births. In a view comparable to the later Christian concept of purgatory as well as the Buddhist karmic hells, in Cicero's 'The Dream of Scipio,' an influential vision of cosmology and the after-life at the end of his De Re Publica, we read that even the worst souls can be purified through horrendous tortures in Tartaros, the lowest pit of the postmortem caverns. Then, chastened, they enter Elysium to await future rebirth. For spirit, the thoughtful Roman lawmaker tells us, is the true self, the only force that moves itself, beginningless and without end.[104]

So it is we are reminded again that the afterlife is divided into several states or 'places' dependent on the qualifications of the deceased, and by and large these become more and more sharply defined as time advances. Although certain prestigious individuals, such as tribal chiefs and Egyptians pharaohs, may have always anticipated an afterlife no less prestigious than their present state, one gradually shared with their most heroic warriors, for most people a common – and often gloomy – postmortem state was the best that could be hoped for. But as time advanced, and especially after the Axial Age, judgment and destiny were increasingly individualized, so that the punishment personally fit the crime, and reward the personal virtue. By Dante's time popes and emperors could languish in hell, and saintly peasants enjoy heaven's rewards.

Yet individual qualifications were, and generally are in religion today, not only moral, but also related to individual faith and ritual preparation. These specifications will be the topic of our next chapter.

Chapter 7

On the Long March: Community and Religious Solidarity vs. Individual Reward and Punishment

Shamans and Saviors

In some early societies, afterlife fate was often not highly differentiated among individuals, but was collective. Deceased children would be reborn in the same family; most persons from the same tribe would take essentially the same journey to the other world, save perhaps for exceptional rulers, shamans, or warriors.

On the other hand, then and much later, rites and initiations, basically reflecting the common beliefs of a community and the power of its collective priests and prayers, could greatly assist in the transition of an individual, so that she or he was not solely dependent on personal virtue. Indeed, the virtue of some individuals, such as saints, redounded to everyone as sources of power. At the same time societies and religions have emphasized strict individual moral judgment, priestly and magical aids (e.g., mummification in ancient Egypt, requiem masses in Roman Catholicism) were also deployed, leaving no possible assistance uninvoked.

Let us first consider shamans. These specialists in the sacred have consistently held a close relationship to the spirits of the dead and their world, both by virtue of individual initiation and through their social role as psychopomp and retriever of lost souls. We have noted that the Thompson River Native American's view of the afterlife included a 'short cut' taken by shamans on missions to guide, or intercept, spirits in their wanderings between the worlds. Among the Goldi people of Siberia, two funeral ceremonies were held. At the first, some seven days after death, the shaman would enter the deceased's home with his drum, search for the soul, capture it, and cause it to enter a cushion-like receptacle called a *fanya*. Then would follow a banquet at which the *fanya* was honored guest, and would be offered brandy.

At the second or great funeral some time later, after several days of further banqueting, drumming, hunting for the soul, and placing it again in the *fanya*, the shaman solemnly addresses the anxious spirit about the difficulties of travel to the other world, then at sunset makes preparations to accompany it on that awesome journey. He sings, dances, paints his face with soot, and invokes his helping spirits, especially a *koori* or long-necked bird, which he must ride for the return journey. Finally, he climbs a notched tree, from which he declares he is able to see the road to the other world. After shamanizing in trance at length, he seats himself on a board representing a sled, together with the deceased's soul in the *fanya* and a basket of food. Spirit dogs are harnessed to the pretend vehicle; a spirit servant accompanies him.

The shaman then sings of his remarkable journey dramatically as he proceeds. At first the going is easy, but difficulties pile up as a great river appears. Only a good shaman can get his precious burden to the other side. Finally, after many vicissitudes, signs of human activity tell him the village of the dead is not far away. When he reaches it, being careful not to speak the name of departed one aloud, he extracts the soul from the *fanya*, entrusting it to the deceased's closest relatives over there, then hastens to return home in the land of the living. When he arrives back, the shamanic ambassador gives greetings and even small gifts from dead relatives to all tribesmen present, then throws the now-empty *fanya* into the fire.[105]

It remains to note that a relationship to the dead is often involved in the selection or initiation of a shaman as well. While shamans may frequently be chosen by the gods, or the office may in effect be hereditary, it is common for the candidate to be contacted or even possessed by the spirit of a past shaman. A Yakut (Siberian) related that he was so spiritually taken when he cooked food at a site which happened to be over a former shaman's grave. Bororo (South American) shamans may be called upon seeing birds; even whole flocks of parrots, mysteriously appear and disappear around them in the wood; birds of course often represent departed souls.

More often, though, the initiating spirit is met only in the course of probationary austerities as a candidate dwells alone in the wild, fasting and meditating as he makes the famous 'vision quest.'[106] An Eskimo shaman told the great Danish explorer Knud Rasmussen, 'All true wisdom is only to be found far form men, out in the great solitude, and it can only be acquired by suffering. Privations and sufferings are the only things that can open a man's mind to that which is hidden from others.'[107]

The key point is that shamanism is both a private path and a public performance. This specialist in the sacred may find his wisdom and his guide out in the great solitude, and may enjoy inner experiences of trance and vision walled off from others, yet at the same time he is a community figure, indeed the spiritual guide of his people, at once priest, psychopomp, and loremaster. The two roles go together; each validates the other; and no doubt each depends on the other for its full enactment. A private shaman would be a mystic or hallucinator; a public shaman without authentic inner experience would be merely a performer, if not a charlatan – as some certainly were.

Was Orpheus originally a shaman, perhaps of Thracian, Scythian, or central Asia provenance, and thus kin to the Goldi shaman and his kind? Was he this sort of ecstatic guide of the deceased as they made their way toward their true and eternal home? It was widely held in older but classic works, such as E. R. Dodds's *The Greeks and the Irrational* and Vittorio Macchioro's *From Orpheus to Paul: A History of Orphism*, that shamanism lay behind the ancient Greek religion of Orphism, possibly the first major Hellenic impulse toward a desirable afterlife open to all. Orphism in turn was said to have been a significant influence on Plato's myths and visions of afterlife – and so finally left its imprint on the afterlife scenarios of the western monotheistic religions, Judaism, Christianity, and Islam.[108] The issue cannot be fully argued here; certainly, as we have seen, there were other influences, especially Zoroastrianism, on the latter three faiths.

It is, however, interesting to track the 'irrational' and visionary side of Greek culture. The Hellenes had long assumed that dreams and ecstasy (literally, 'standing outside' oneself) conveyed valid knowledge, whether from out of the depths of one's own soul or from external sources. Pindar, already mentioned, wrote: 'When the body is active, the soul sleeps, and when the body sleeps the soul reveals decisions for good and evil by means of dreams.'[109]

An Orphic golden leaflet, found in a late tomb but in Macchioro's opinion very ancient in content, and no doubt of visionary or ecstatic origin, directs the deceased thus: 'In the dwelling of Hades you will find a spring on your left, and near it a white cypress; be careful not to approach this spring. You will find another from which flow cool waves from Lake Mnemosyne (lake of memory). Before you are guardians. To them you will say, "I am the child of Gaea and Uranus (the earth and the sky) and thus belong to a celestial race, as even you must know. Thirst wears and devours me, but give me at once of the refreshing wave which runs from Lake Mnemosyne." And they will give you to drink of the divine spring and from then on you will rule with the heroes.'[110]

It would be easy to compare a text like this – of which the key saying has been more poetically translated and widely reproduced as 'I am a child of earth and starry heaven, but my race is of heaven (alone)'[111] – with the Platonic and Neoplatonic doctrines of the dual earthy and spiritual nature of humankind, and of salvation as a matter of recollecting (*anamnesis*) of our true nature as inwardly spirit, even as the point of Plato's famous myth of the cave is that we here see only shadows cast by greater reality, but an escape into the light that was really there all the time is possible. Gnostic Christianity best perpetuated this version of salvation into the new faith, but hints of it linger in the canonical New Testament, especially in Paul and John: 'For although they knew God they did not honor him as God or give thanks to him, but they became futile in their thinking and their senseless minds were darkened' (Rom. 1:22).

Ecstatic religion has sometimes focused on possession. Here is an account from J. H. Chajes, *Between Worlds; Dybbuks, Exorcists, and Early Modern Judaism*. (A dybbuk is the soul of a demon or dead person who enters the body of a living person and controls that individual.)

> In the early 1540s, a Jewish boy in the Galilean – and, for nearly a generation, Ottoman – village of Safed [an important center of Kabbalistic thought], was possessed by the soul of a sinner, a dybbuk. Furious that the boy's father had killed the dog in which he had formerly been lodged, the soul sought vengeance by killing the man's son. The eminent sage who was called upon to exorcise the spirit, having forced it to speak with threats of excommunication, discovered that there was little he could do but rescue the boy by removing the intruder and banishing him to the wilderness. This he accomplished by intoning a classic Hebrew liturgical formula, though with a magical twist: the rabbi recited the words both forward and backward.[112]

Note that the episode presumed *gilgul*, the Kabbalistic concept of reincarnation. The offending spirit was not a demon, as it might have been earlier, but a deceased human being who, for his sins, had been reincarnated in a dog.

Safedic possessing spirits were not all malicious, nor were all adepts at their management male. Hayyim Vital, a preeminent student of the great Kabbalist Isaac Luria, tells us in his diary – a rare and important work – of a 'wise woman,' Soñadora, who as a 'dreamer' and expert in the art of oil-gazing was able to foretell the future. Vital relates that on one occasion in 1570, as she chanted while scanning the mysteriously changing liquid, Soñadora was at first unable to respond, but then 'she was imbued [*lit*. enclothed] by a zealous spirit, and strengthened herself in her incantations. She then stood on her feet, and kissed my feet . . .' The seeress was then able to perceive the letters formed by the oil, and on that basis was able to tell the inquirer of his greatness of soul and promising future in mystic learning.[113]

Religious venues featuring spirit-possession are virtually as common today as in the sixteenth century. As so often, in practice the lines between gods, demons, and spirits of the human departed are frequently blurred, as is any technical distinction between medium, seer, and shaman. The author once visited a seance in a Spiritualist church in a suburb of Los Angeles. Some twenty people sat in a circle with the medium in a darkened room. The medium, a mature Spiritualist minister, went into trance with a series of four pronounced jerks; speaking again, his voice had noticeably changed. As was his custom, he gave messages from a series of four spirits: a temperamental Hindu philosopher, deep and ponderous; Harry, a hoarse-voiced 'common man'; and two Native Americans, the 'Indian guides' routinely invoked in Spiritualism, one serious, the other full of folk humor. The Hindu and Harry answered metaphysical questions; the two others brought messages from spirits of loved ones and told details of the furnishings of one's house and one's personal life, at times quite accurately. These speakers were presumably deceased human beings, though perhaps from ages ago, but functionally they could have been gods or angels.

The same minister once told me that, as a child on a farm in Illinois, he had experienced a series of seizures during which strange voices spoke through him. His parents were understandably concerned, but finally a Spiritualist minister had recognized them as spirit voices. They then resolved themselves into the four voices which have been his 'controls' ever since. This happened in the twentieth century; it might have been the call of a paleolithic shaman.

Spiritualism and related phenomena are found worldwide; they take particularly colorful form in certain Afro-American movements in

Latin America, such as Voudon in Haiti and Louisiana, Santería in Cuba and the United States, Macumba and Candomblé in Brazil. I once visited a Voudon (Voodoo) ceremony in New Orleans. As the brightly-dressed *mambo* (priestess) was possessed by a *loa* (deity), she more and more performed the distinctive dance of that figure; often priests (*houngan*) or mambo will not only speak in a distinctive accent, but smoke cigars or drink quantities of rum, if such are the attributes of the possessing deity, even if the vehicle is quite abstemious otherwise.

In shamanism, Kabbalism, Spiritualism, Voudon, and the rest, it is clear that spiritual power is obtained through identification with otherworldly spirits, however vaguely defined, and that this is a public as well as a private performance, exercised for both the admiration and benefit of a community. But what of the other side of religion, the sanctioning of moral and ethical values? How do they prepare one for the afterlife, or even for rapprochement with the Supreme Spirit?

Moral Qualifications

The weighing of the heart (or soul) in the ancient Egyptian after-death scenario has been mentioned. To the Egyptians, the heart, not the brain, was the seat of emotion, and also of morality. After death, the heart was examined by Anubis, the mortuary god, then taken to the presence of Osiris, where it was weighed on a scales against a feather representing Maat, the moral order. If the heart was heavier, the deceased was unprepared for a blissful afterlife. Here, it seems, one's moral weight must be the deciding factor.

Yet not entirely. As we have seen, the ancient Egyptian preparation for the afterlife involved much more than a good moral and ethical life: spells had to be imparted to ward off demons, maps of the other world displayed as guides, mummification practiced in apparent belief that a well-preserved body on this side benefited one's journey on the other, and so it goes. Regarding the confusing melange Egyptian religion can seem to present, one writer commented, 'The impression made on the modern mind is that of a people searching in the dark for a key to truth and, having found not one but many keys resembling the pattern of the lock, retaining all lest perchance the appropriate one should be discarded.'[114]

Many keys proposing to fit the lock await the modern seeker as well. The sociologist of religion Nancy T. Ammerman has recently studied what she calls 'Golden Rule Christianity.' This attitude, very commonly found on Main Street U.S.A. and in the more liberal to 'mainstream' churches, says it doesn't matter what one believes or to what congregation one belongs, so long as one lives in accordance with the Golden Rule: 'Do unto others as you would have others do unto you,' seen as a shorthand for basic morality.[115]

Yet, though there may be some non-church-going Golden Rule Christians for whom this attitude is close to sufficient, Ammerman found that numerous Golden Rulers do also attend churches wherein which they say prayers based on faith as well as morality, profess to believe the Bible in some sense (after all, it is in it that sacred book the Golden Rule is found: Matt. 7:12, Luke 6:31), and use the church for life's basic ceremonies.

In particular, one could add, like the ancient Egyptians these moderns surround death with not one but many practices, whether all are mutually consistent or not. While attitude and practice are changing in some quarters, in most parts of the world, including the 'Golden Rule' heartland, elaborate, often expensive, funeral rites are observed, and seemingly meet some deeply felt need. While one may not go quite so far as mummification, in Britain and the United States artful embalming and luxurious caskets or cremation vessels are often desired, as are costly tombstones or memorial plaques, and the funeral service may well be replete with prayers for the deceased in his or her transition between worlds, as well as for the well-being of the survivors. It is common also to have a wake or funeral feast of some sort, and until fairly recently distinctive mourning clothes were worn and wreaths hung.

All this, of course, is as much for the benefit of survivors as for the deceased; the beauty and elegance of the service aiding catharsis for grief, and mental transition to a new generation. Death is not a private matter alone, but involves family and community. Insofar as the latter means the religious community, it entails those rites, and implied beliefs, by which that community defines its identity and by the same token draws its boundaries.

In other words, in the last analysis communities – however liberal in belief – acknowledge that in this world morality alone is not enough. The Golden rule is insufficient to meet the ultimate needs confronted in death. Moreover, many of us, if honest, realize that morality alone can be exceedingly ambivalent. Knowing the right thing to do can be excruciating difficult, and even more problematically, when perhaps we *do* know, we may ruefully concur with St. Paul when he said, 'I do not understand my own actions . . . For I do not do the good I want, but the evil I would not do is what I do' (Rom. 7: 15, 19).

Or, we may well identify with Arjuna's complaint in the Bhagavad-Gita. After listening to Krishna instruct him at length on the virtue of following dharma, the pattern of right living – broadly speaking, the moral and ethical values appropriate to one's place in society – including karma-yoga, good action done for its own sake, without attachment to the fruits of action, the prince wonders if that is enough, or even possible:

> Suppose a man has faith, but does not struggle hard enough? His mind wanders away from the practice of yoga and he fails to reach perfection. What will become of him then?
>
> When a man goes astray from the path to Brahman, he has missed both lives, the worldly and the spiritual. He has no support anywhere. Is he not lost, as a broken cloud is lost in the sky?[116]

In other words, a person who, like St. Paul, tries the way of faith and virtue, but discovers that what he would do he does not, and what he would not do that he does, would seem to have the worst of both worlds – neither a life of true spirituality nor a plain worldly life with all its pleasures. Is there any hope for such a person?

Krishna says in fact there is. Greater than mortification, greater than learning, greater even than good works, is simple worship, loving self-surrender despite one's faults:

> He gives me all his heart,
> He worships me in faith and love:
> That yogi, above every other,
> I call my very own.[117]

In the concept of God, in worship (*bhakti* or devotion to God is implied), in the very idea of yoga, a religious community, with its traditional language and practice, is indicated. Religion apart from human community is hardly imaginable. Those who say they can live only by Golden Rule morality, and can worship alone in the midst of nature, need to realize that the very words by which one says this to oneself stem from language. Our language was not individually invented, but taught in the context of family and community. Without community, even without language like those feral children occasion-ally discovered, one could presumably have experiences which might be interpreted as religious by those who know such words as 'God' and 'blessing,' but would not be so named by them, they having no such language-tools. On the other hand, shared religious belief not only interiorizes meanings for feelings and realizations, but also provides a shared bond, forged of similar self-definitions, that makes a community.

At first the bond was no doubt within a clan or tribe, then a larger social order like that defined by the Hindu concept of dharma or the Christendom of medieval Europe. Although flexible in the sense of providing different ways of relating to the universe for people of various schools and classes, it was difficult if not impossible to opt out of the system as a whole. As Wilfred Cantwell Smith has emphasized, the contemporary idea of 'a religion' as something individual and optional, thereby different from a traditional social order with its gods and humans both in their proper places, is a fairly modern idea. Even the word 'religion,' in anything like its current meaning, does not have an equivalent in most pre-modern languages: the Sanskrit *dharma*, like the Chinese *dao*, does not really bespeak what we now call a 'religion.'[118] They indicate something more like, 'The way our world works as a secular/sacred unity,' or 'What you need to know – about world, rites, community, family – to live well in our society.'

Only since early modern times, and only after much pain and difficulty, have we come to think of 'a religion' as not integral to its environing social order, but instead as a personal, elective, and detachable part of that order, with its own separate institutions, which one can adhere to or not without forfeiting one's role in the secular aspects of the same society; the separation is still not entirely perfect. Even so, those 'religions,' or if one prefer denominations, are themselves communities. One may belong simultaneously to several communities today – work, avocational, family, as well as religious. But within the faith option, religious language is still interiorized and shared; it could not be otherwise.

Henri Bergson declared that the two sources of morality and religion were what he called the static and the dynamic: the need of a society to integrate and maintain itself through sacred sanctions for its values and moral code; and the dynamic side of religion expressed in prophesy and mysticism.[119] The two, as we have seen, ultimately sustain and validate each other, and the duality carries over to deathbed and afterlife. It is said one dies alone, but from the point of view of religion this is not truly the case.

In Evelyn Waugh's celebrated novel *Brideshead Revisited*, the worldly old Lord Marchmain lies dying, barely conscious, and a priest strives finally to reconcile him to God and the church. The cleric said to him, ' "I know you are sorry for all the sins of your life, aren't you? Make a sign, if you can. You're sorry, aren't you?" But there was no sign.' The priest commenced absolution anyway: *Ego te absolvo in nomine Patris* . . . He began to administer final unction. Then, suddenly, the dying reprobate raised a hand, made the sign of the cross. The sign was given; then he was soon gone from this world.[120] It was only one man and a country priest, but two is community, confirmed by its symbols of language and gesture, and behind them and the cleric lay a mighty institution with a long tradition. Lord Marchmain had lived life his own way, but he did not die alone.

Chapter 8

Amazing Grace: The Difficult vs. the Easy Path

How Much Is Enough?

Though of a different religion, here is a medieval Japanese Pure Land Buddhist who would have recognized and respected Lord Marchmain's reconciliation to grace at the last possible moment. Then as now, there were those contemptuous of deathbed forgiveness after a lifetime of sin. But Shinran (1173–1263), founder of the True Pure Land faith (Jodo Shinshu) emphasized that salvation was not by one's own good works, but purely by the grace – assistance or power – of Amida Buddha, who as we have seen vowed that all who call upon his name in faith will be saved out of his infinite compassion. He reportedly said that even one recitation of the *nembutsu* – the chant *Namu Amida Butsu*, 'Hail Amida Buddha,' by which one affirmed this faith – was enough, even if that one chant was on a deathbed.

For it was not by much reciting that one was brought into Amida's Pure Land. Indeed, too much piety might induce one to rely vaingloriously on one's own faith rather than Amida's power. Shinran went so far as to remark that although some argue, if even a wicked person can be reborn in the Pure Land, how much more a good person, it's really the other way around: if even a good person can be reborn in the Pure Land, how much more a wicked person, for, 'Amida made his vow with the intention of bringing wicked men to Buddhahood. Therefore the wicked man who depends on the power of another [Amida] is the prime object of Salvation.'[121]

Shinran has been called the Martin Luther of Japan, and he resembles the great Protestant reformer in several respects, from his insistence on salvation by divine grace received through faith alone, to his recognition that, in such a dispensation, monastic vows, including celibacy and other austerities, were of no particular avail; both the Christian and the Buddhist gave up monkhood, married, and begat children. Yet the comparison with Lord Marchmain's priest is not spurious in the present context, for all – the Pure Land Buddhist, the Protestant, the Catholic – were convinced that, in extremis, all that really counted was a simple, one-time act of faith: a three word chant, a prayer, the sign of the cross. That was enough to open floodgates of grace sufficient to carry one over into the land of light and glory.

Doing It the Hard Way

Yet in other traditions, adequate preparation for the afterlife requires not only strict morality, but also arduous regimens of yoga, initiation, and pilgrimage which change an individual into virtually another being, one more capable of deathlessness. Take for example the Yoga Sutras, presenting the eight 'limbs' or aspects of the path based on the practice of yogas or spiritual disciplines of body and mind. In its present form this text probably derives from the very early centuries C.E. It draws from India's deeply biological, psychosomatic understanding of human nature as the background for liberation. Hatha-yoga, the physical yoga of posture and breathing exercises, plays a major role in the spiritual quest. Rightly understood, breath and body are indispensable tools. Brought under control of spirit as precision instruments, they can facilitate states of consciousness that evoke the goals of spirit.

The quest of the *yogi*, the practitioner of yoga, is to control of the modulations of mind – in other words, it is to reach *kaivalya*, 'isolation,' of the true self or spirit, as the adept wins independence from the anxiety and limitations imposed by interaction with the changing world of sight, feeling, and fantasy. This is done by getting mind and body strictly under control by discipline of flesh, breath, and thought, then using this control to withdraw attention from the outer world, so the inner light shines unimpeded.

According to the Yoga Sutras, the process comprises eight steps, or 'limbs.' The first two, *yama* and *niyama*, are positive and negative moral rules aimed at a life of quietness, gentleness, and purity, for one's manner of life must be prepared and purified before yoga can hope to succeed. Releasing yoga's potent spiritual force into an unworthy vessel can, in fact, be dangerous both to the individual and to society. Yama inculcates abstention from harming others, from lying, from stealing, from lack of self-control, and from covetousness. Remarkable claims are made for these simple precepts. If one truly practices harmlessness (ahimsa), all living creatures will approach him without fear. If one abjures theft, all wealth will flow toward him. (Perhaps the intent is like that of Jesus' saying, 'And every one who has left houses or brothers or sisters or father or mother or children or lands, for my name's sake, will receive a hundredfold, and inherit eternal life'; Matt. 19:29.)

Then come the two limbs of *asana* (posture) and *pranayama* (breath control) in which the psychosomatic powers are lined up to move in the one direction of liberation. After the *yogi* gains control of his or her own bodily and emotional house in this way, *pratyahara*, the stage of disengagement from outer things, becomes possible. *Pratyahara* is withdrawal from the outward-directed senses and their objects, so that one in this state does not *really* see, hear, or feel.

We might think such a person would be at a great disadvantage, but the converse is true, according to Patanjali. *Pratyahara* clears the way for acute inner, subtle ways of awareness. Just as a blind person develops especially sharp senses of touch and hearing, so yoga tells us that when all the gross senses are withdrawn, other undreamed-of capabilities latent in the human being begin to stir. When they come to be mastered, the *yogi* has clairvoyant awareness of things near and far and the ability to use occult forces, beside which the ordinary senses and capacities are as an oxcart to a rocketship.

The Yoga Sutras also tell us how to read minds, walk on water, fly through the air, make oneself as tiny as an atom, and become impervious to hunger and thirst. But these powers, called *siddhis*, while doubtless tempting to many, are to be given up for an even greater goal – true liberation of the true self. This is the work of the last three stages, called Raja Yoga because by them one becomes as it were king in one's own house, in one's body and mind. They are interior: *dharana*, concentration; *dhyana*, meditation; and *samadhi*, the absolutely equalized consciousness of perfect freedom. The practitioner learns how to focus the mind on one thing: 'one-pointed' meditation. That concentration can be expanded to become true deep meditation or *dhyana*. Finally, the flow of mind smooths out to become *samadhi*, evenness of thought, which in turn means *kaivalya* or isolation of true mind in the midst of all the clutter around.[122]

The Way of Merit

It might be argued that, in a real sense, the previously mentioned 'Golden Rule Christianity,' asserting the important thing is not belief but good morality, if taken seriously would no less be a 'hard way' than yoga. Good deeds are not always easy to perform, and exact reciprocity toward others whether you like them or not can be much harder than praying and leaving it to God. In Christianity, the heresy that one has complete free will and is judged on the basis of one's good or evil works is called Pelagianism (after the Celtic monk Pelagius, d. 418). St. Augustine, and later Luther and Calvin, battled mightily against this doctrine, insisting that one cannot do good – or even believe aright or have right faith – apart from God's prior grace. Nevertheless Pelagianism is undoubtedly the practical doctrine of the Golden Rulers, and of a great many other persons who take for granted that whether you go to heaven or hell depends on how your sins and merits balance out. This rough-and-ready doctrine has a place in the lay religion, particularly, of most faiths.

In Buddhism, especially the Theravada Buddhism of Southeast Asia, the practice of most laypeople is primarily concerned with making sufficient 'merit,' or good karma, to ensure a good incarnation in one's next birth, perhaps even as a deva in one of the delightful heavens. Merit is won by following the five basic precepts – do not kill, steal, lie, engage in sexual immorality, or take intoxicants – leading up to the four 'unlimited' virtues: unlimited friendliness, compassion, sympathetic joy, and equanimity of mind. But meritorious deeds also include activities of a more ritual nature: building pagodas, presenting traditional offerings of flowers and fruit, giving robes to the monks, and food to them after the rainy-season retreat.

Buddhism has another level as well, as we know: doing the straight-dealing vipassana meditations of analysis that lead directly to Nirvana, not simply to a better rebirth. That is the ultimate goal. Often even merit-making is presented as preparing one not just for a better rebirth in worldly terms, but for rebirth as a monk prepared to become a *sotapanna* or 'stream-enterer' assured of liberation after seven lifetimes, or even as an arhat in his last lifetime. Many lay practices offer such an auspicious rebirth, but only after ninety-nine lives. Yet the idea of a 'split-level' personal eschatology is clear.

A parallel, though not identical, view was the case in medieval Catholicism in Europe, as it has been in modern Roman Catholicism.

The basic requirement is avoiding mortal sin, or if committed confessing the mortal sin and receiving absolution. Unforgiven mortal sin at the time of death could only lead to hell. Although common lists of the 'Seven Deadly Sins' – pride, envy, wrath, sloth, greed, gluttony, and lust – provide psychological insight in sin, in practice a mortal sin is generally seen as a grave violation of one of the ten commandments as expounded by Catholic moralists: for example, missing mass breaks the fourth, about honoring the Sabbath; and murder, including abortion, breaks the seventh commandment, 'Thou shalt not kill.' So it was that a person free of mortal sin, even if still bearing venial or minor sin, could eventually reach heaven, though it may be only after an extended sojourn in Purgatory.

Just as a few Theravada Buddhists of very high spiritual attainment could reach enlightenment comparable to that of the Buddha himself, so some Catholic saints knew ecstatic and mystical experiences that brought them near the gates of heaven in this life. Not a few also were capable of visions and miracles. All this was regarded as extraordinary graces which God bestowed on certain favored individuals, perhaps as a sign to the world, but such extraordinary faculties are not necessary for salvation. Only in heaven will all have the beatific vision of God's immediate presence.

Stages of the Spiritual Life

Just as Patanjali's yoga presented its series of 'limbs,' and comparable stages of spiritual growth can be found in Buddhist and Islamic Sufi literature, so the Catholic Christian advance to mystic blessedness and sainthood had its steps, outlined by such classic spiritual writers as St. John of the Cross and St. Teresa of Avila. A convenient synthesis and summary of this literature is found in Evelyn Underhill's influential work, *Mysticism*.[123]

Underhill distinguishes five basic stages: Awakening, Preparation or Purgation, Illumination, the 'Dark Night of the Soul,' and the Unitive State. Awakening, the beginning of the spiritual path, the way in which one is called to set foot on it, is immensely varied from one person to another. Some may have an apparently sudden and spontaneous opening, like being 'born again' or seeing an unearthly light. St. Catherine of Genoa, when 26 and depressed from an unhappy marriage, was suddenly caught up in an overflowing experience of divine love and her own inadequacy while making her confession to a saintly priest.

On the other side of the world, the Chinese Buddhist monk Maozi Yuan found his thirst of enlightenment aroused by hearing the cry of a crow in the middle of the night. St. Francis of Assisi heard the painted lips of a crucifix in a dilapidated chapel telling him to repair his church – a command he first took literally, and then realized it had a far broader meaning, to be inaugurated in his new order of dedicated friars.

Awakening, however, is not enough. More than one aspirant has been powerfully invigorated by an emotional awakening, and then weakened as its intensity has worn off. So it is that spiritual teachers admonish that regular spiritual discipline must come next to channel those energies into deep, habitual practices. It is like directing over-flowing flood-waters into straight irrigation ditches whereby they will saturate the growing plants regularly and in the right amount. This is a period when it is important to follow a precise and regular spiritual discipline of prayer, meditation, yoga, chanting – whatever suits one's own path – whether one always feels like it or not, for the point is it should become habitual, not dependent on moods and feelings. This is the Preparatory or Purgative stage, the latter term suggesting that it not only establishes good habits, but also helps cleanse away those negative usages, perhaps even addictions, belonging to the former life.

In time, the flowers planted, watered, and well cultivated in the Preparatory stage burst into bloom. The Illuminative stage is essentially a happy time of religious satisfaction: of prayers answered, blessings received, rich experience in worship, the presence of God near at hand. It may take different forms for different persons, and in different traditions, but in all cases it is a divine consummation of Awakening and Preparation. For many people, it is what religion is supposed to be all about, and is enough.

There are some, however, who go on to something more. At first the next stage seems far more negative than rewarding. An unexpected, and very unpleasant, feeling of emptiness indwelling what had until now seemed spiritual fulfillment arises. Prayers and prostrations are mere hollow forms, and God in his true reality is hidden or withdrawn. Mantras or meditations are only dry springs, not the fountains of grace they once were. Some may assume at this point that religion was after all only an illusion, and give up.

But this is the stage described by St. John of the Cross (1542–1591) in his monumental work, *The Dark Night of the Soul*. The Dark Night is actually another, higher level of Purgation, designed to prepare one for even greater fulfillment.[124] It is intended to cleanse the aspirant of attachment even to the fruits of religion itself.

For there is danger, first, in thinking that in the blessings of the Illuminative state you have 'arrived,' that your beliefs and practices are all there is and God himself could lead you no further. Yet the chances are those beliefs and practices are so intertwined with your self-identity, and perhaps also the religious and cultural nexus with which you also identify yourself, as to become a subtle form of egotism. This is something to be purged away.

Second, one can become attached to spiritual experiences of pleasures. They can become habitual, even addictive, like those of the table or the bottle. One's spiritual life may become itself a kind of fascination, even a hobby. But when what had been means of grace become themselves empty and dry, and you feel alone on a desert at midnight without a light except the distant stars, you know you need a new start free of spiritual attachments.

When that freedom has been won, the pilgrim is ready to enter the state of oneness with the divine, the Unitive State, the highest of Underhill's five. Here union is not dependent on particular practices, though they may be used, for the presence of God is now deep down and continual, expressed now not so much in thinking *about* God, as simply in a general sense of well-being and inner joy one may have. Any dualism of God and self has been overcome. St. Teresa of Avila, with her usual subtle perceptiveness, writes of a union with God in which the soul is aware of union and 'rejoicing in its captivity' – the Illuminative state. Then she describes an even higher state in which 'there is no sense of anything but enjoyment, without any knowledge of what is being enjoyed,' and yet the soul now 'enjoys incomparably more' in contemplative prayer, without any words or ideas coming between the mystic and complete union.[125]

Another great mystical writer, Meister Eckhart, put it in his pungently paradoxical way when he preached that we must 'pray that we may be rid of God, and taking the truth, break into eternity' where we exist in simple desireless being as in the womb, knowing God truly by being rid of the *idea* of God.[126]

This seems also the Buddhist Nirvana, the Sufi *fana* or 'falling away' into God, the Yogic realization of *samadhi* and *kaivalya*. These are all experiences that seem to require the long, though no doubt richly rewarding, practice of a step-by-step discipline to reach – though it should be emphasized that these teachers do not see them as at all mechanical; Underhill tells us that some seekers may do her five stages in different orders, or even skip one, or experience two more or less simultaneously; the spiritual life is far more an art, like learning to paint or play the piano, than a science.

In any case, for us the upshot is that, attaining the mind of Union or Nirvana, one is already in effect in the afterlife as understood on this rarefied plane, and simply continues on in it after physical death. The others, for whom it is a simple matter of faith, almost instantaneous when the act of faith is made, might say that life for the believer is no different than for the unitive mystic, though it be in the midst of everyday life.

Is the Unitive State – call it that, or attaining Nirvana or Enlightenment or God-realization – something to be achieved through serious effort or dedication, even if one acknowledge it is also, or entirely, a work of divine grace at base? Or is it possible for perfection to come effortlessly, or for a chosen one simply to be born with it? This is too complex an issue to be resolved here, and in any case strictly speaking pertains more to the saint's life in this world than to the afterlife, though of course has ramifications on the other side. It might be useful to point out, however, that Hinduism makes a distinction between a *jivanmukta*, a liberated or, in the common term, 'God-realized' human being, and an *avatar*, a 'descent' or, loosely speaking, incarnation of a god in human form.

Tales of the latter, like the infant Krishna or, more recently, Satya Sai Baba (b. 1926), considered an avatar by numerous followers, emphasize their sinless perfection and miracle-working capacity from infancy on up. Although they may display a childish mischievousness, as in the famous story of the toddler Krishna's stealing the butter, causing his mother to try to tie him up in punishment, their pranks are with a point – the exasperated mother found that no matter how much rope she used, her divine son could no more be tied than the infinite God can be circumscribed by human reason or merit; only through love is God known.

In the same way, Christians, regarding the one incarnation in which they believe, God incarnate in Jesus Christ, would maintain he was as perfect as God from conception on: some doctrine holds even his birth was painless, and in the words of the familiar hymn, even in the manger, 'no crying he makes.' Likewise, his one recorded 'prank,' staying behind in the temple on a family pilgrimage to Jerusalem to talk with the learned doctors, was with a point – to show that he 'must be about his Father's business.'

But as for saints and enlightened beings who have progressed from a state like ours to fulfillment, the picture in traditional accounts (not to mention modern revisionist histories) is a little different. For some, like St. Paul or St. Augustine, or the Tibetan Milarepa, who practiced black magic against an evil uncle before realizing this was not the true Buddhist way, dramatic conversion from sin is the crux of the story.[127] But even in the case of those who gave evidence of special calling early in life, enough was lacking to make meaningful further development. St. Teresa of Avila, beautiful and vivacious in her youth, greatly enjoyed dancing and mild flirtations, pastimes we might consider reasonably innocent in a teenage girl, though she later condemned them as worldly. St. Francis was likewise a high-spirited and impulsive youth before he heard words from the painted Christ of that dilapidated chapel, and transferred his unbounded energy and emotionality to the service of rebuilding his church.

Ramakrishna (1836–1886), the revered modern Hindu holy man, showed marked intelligence and memory, as well as a basic goodness of heart, from a very early age. He could, it is said, retain long hymns to the gods even after one hearing. Yet he had no taste for school-learning, particularly mathematics, often falling into deep meditation – a fore-taste of his later pattern – when he should have been studying. He engaged in the same sort of boisterous shenanigans as other boys, but differed from them in that, instead of making excuses when caught, he freely confessed, though this was no guarantee that he would not do the same again. Yet his gentle nature usually prevailed in the end, and he did no serious harm to anyone.[128] Some called him an avatar like Krishna.

Those who attain to these highest rungs of the spiritual life, whether by faith, transformative effort, or auspicious birth, clearly are already in his life where they will continue to be in the next. The spiritual path starts here and keeps on going through the doorway of death.

Chapter 9

The End of Days: Linear and Cyclical Time

The Beginning and the End

The western monotheistic religions, together with popular eastern views of reincarnation, indicate both history and personal time are moving toward a future goal, though it may be as near as the other side of one's deathbed or as far as the end of the age. But cyclical models, like the primal Australian perspective that sees life rotating between world and Dreamtime, or the Platonic and Hindu four declining ages, suggest the nature of one's life is conditioned by where one is in the cycle, here or there, high or low. All this is reflected in myths both philosophical and popular.

Some traditional cultures have a concept of a primal Golden Age, followed by a catastrophe leading to worse, then a long slide down to the present. In the earliest myths, however, humans often first emerged miserably as the gods' scum or slaves, while the heavens rang with divine warfare. In Greek mythology, all these prospects seem to have obtained: some poets sang of a Golden Age, but others saw mortals as no more than playthings of the gods, frequently objects of their temperamental anger, not possessing even fire till it was given them by Prometheus in defiance of Zeus. Those humans fortunate enough to live in a primal Golden Age or Eden enjoyed harmony with nature and with one another, as is suggested by Adam's naming of the animals, and had a specific job to do, such as Adam and Eve's tending of the blessed garden.[129]

We will look at these beliefs and their mythology in terms of those several categories. First will be those based on a linear view of time: that time moves forward like an arrow in one direction, from beginning to end. In such religions as the western monotheistic faiths,

Judaism, Christianity, and Islam, that means essentially marching straight down the millennia from Creation to the Last Judgment. In the orthodox perspective of these traditions, the End may also include the resurrection of the dead: the deceased buried or cremated, whether in earth or sea, rise again in full physical body to face their Maker and receive their verdict. One interesting variation is the Rapture, popular in some evangelical Christian circles: belief that the truly faithful righteous will be taken up to Heaven before that Day of Days.

Another widespread picture is of the Earthly Paradise: visions of places on this earth like Shambhala or Camelot which now, or in the past, or to come, anticipate on the terrestrial plane the future paradise. If one believe in the Garden of Eden and the Fall of Adam and Eve, it is also a recapitulation of the prelapsarian primal paradise. Indeed, a theme we will commonly find is that, in the eschatological scenarios of linear time, the End is in the Beginning. Just as Christ, as Savior, is Second Adam, so the final paradise resembles nothing so much as the first Eden, restored as though the disaster had never happened. Eastern versions also obtain, especially in Buddhist movements centered around Maitreya, the coming future Buddha and his paradise. Examples include the revolutionary White Lotus Society in China, to be considered later, and some of the New Religions of Japan.

These paradisal dreams have not been the province of religion alone. Another thread running through human imagination: secular versions of eschatology, even of apocalyptic, and of the earthly paradise. Over and over, visionaries have dreamed of an earthly paradise constructed essentially of human thought and effort, or just occurring by some sort of fortuitous chance: Avalon, Platonic republics, utopias. After the idea of progress took firm hold by the eighteenth century, the earthly paradise came to be thought of as the ultimate end of the farthest-out advances in science, philosophy, and democracy, when earth would be fair, and all its dwellers brave and free.

One intellectual lineage saw this eschatological wonder as the product of gradual social evolution, but another school, more impatient, brought forth a secular version of apocalyptic in the notion of revolution: when conditions got bad enough, the people would overthrow the evil old order in one mighty spasm of upheaval, and produce a secular-millennial kingdom of justice and plenty, in which the state itself might wither away. But the revolution of course was violent, like an apocalypse with its Four Horsemen and its Shaking of the Foundations; thousands, even millions, might die that the other thousands or millions might enter the kingdom. This vision long haunted the world, above all in the two centuries between the French revolution of 1789 and the collapse of Russian communism, a later fruit of that secular apocalyptic vision, in 1989.

Then there are the cyclical visions of time and their relation to eschatology. As we will see, they are not quite as non-linear, at least on the short-term, as might be thought. But whether Platonic in the West or Hindu and Buddhist in the East, they cast light of another color on the process. Characteristically, the cycle begins with a Golden Age, then degenerates through lesser eras to a final evil condition, the Iron Age or Kaliyuga, when life is short and brutish, before the dissolution of the present world and the beginning of the cycle again. Finally, we will take a look at the interesting idea of eternal recurrence, made famous by Friedrich Nietzsche but with roots in the ancient cycles, which seems oddly to mediate between linear and cyclical time, and between the secular and the sacred.

'The Ultimate Trip'

This is the title of a chapter in *The Late Great Planet Earth* by Hal Lindsay, a book which sold millions of copies after its first publication in 1970, and became a touchstone of the evangelical-apocalyptic revival of the late twentieth century – a movement which could be said to have begun with this book and the post–1960s 'Jesus People' trend among young people, and to have culminated in the also bestselling end-of-millennium 'Left Behind' series of novels by Tim LaHaye and Jerry B. Jenkins.[130] Against the dramas of the Cold War, the Moon landing, the civil rights and antiwar confrontations in the 1960s generation, and the gradual rising of secular awareness of ecological and climate-change issues, these works posited the imminence of a drama to trump them all: divine intervention, and the last days of planet Earth as we know it.

No small part of that drama was the Rapture. Here are Hal Lindsay's words:

It will happen!
Someday, a day that only God knows, Jesus Christ is coming to take away all those who believe in Him. He is coming to meet all true believers in the air. Without benefit of science, space suits, or interplanetary rockets, there will be those who will be transported into a glorious place more beautiful, more awesome, than we can

possible comprehend. Earth and all its thrills, excitement, and pleasures will be nothing in contrast to this great event.

It will be the living end. The ultimate trip.[131]

Here are a couple of fictionalized raptures, according to Lindsay:

'There I was, driving down the freeway and all of a sudden the place went crazy . . . cars going in all directions . . . and not one of them had a driver. I mean it was wild! I think we've got an invasion from outer space!'

'It was puzzling – very puzzling. I was teaching my course in the Philosophy of Religion when all of a sudden three of my students vanished. They simply vanished! They were quite argumentative – always trying to prove their point from the Bible. No great loss to the class. However, I do find this disappearance very difficult to explain.'[132]

Glenn W. Shuck, in *Marks of the Beast: The Left Behind Novels and the Struggle for Evangelical Identity*, suggests that while this kind of apocalyptic, whether from Lindsay or LaHaye/Jenkins, may be off the radar of most intellectuals – just as the Rapture was clearly not part of the former's professor of Philosophy of Religion's world of expectations – it is not pointless and its popular culture meaning must be understood.[133] What apocalyptic does is, like all myth, deal with the great issues of our present existence in history in story form – in this case, future as well as past story. These were times when many ordinary people felt confused by a rapidly changing world in which their inner lives seemed lost in an abstraction of bureaucracy and innumerable new technologies, and of changing lifestyles which truly seemed to leave the person of traditional values behind. They yearned instead to be part of something important, to have a significant part in a great drama. In the vast theater of Christian apocalyptic even humble believers could see their faithfulness honored with starring roles in the Rapture, and on this stage even the halt and the lame could fight as front-line soldiers in the battle against the Beast. A world of colorless ambiguity could be turned upside down, and inside out.

Note, however, that this ultimate drama is nonetheless close to our world: it could happen any day, on our ordinary highways, homes, or classrooms. In the same way, the ultimate trip is oddly continuous with ours in geography too. The New Testament Book of Revelation, on which much of such modern 'prophecy' is based, contains actual, transvalued, allegorical, and purely non-earthly locations: the actual Isle of Patmos in the Aegean Sea, where the revelation was received; Jerusalem, this-worldly but transformed into the Heavenly City; Babylon, the city mother of all wickedness, clearly standing in for Rome, and places entirely otherwhere, like the throne set up in heaven and the bottomless pit.[134] (In the same way, in China the Isles of the Blest lie off the east coast, even as Shambhala and the Western Paradise are hidden somewhere amid the vast mountain ranges and deserts of central Asia. Both are continuous with the Middle Kingdom's geography yet also detached, sometimes visible and sometimes not.)

Christian eschatology has divided into two wings, post-millennialist and pre-millennialist. The millennium is the thousand-year reign of Christ predicted in Revelation chapter 20, after which Satan must be released from his bondage for a little while before the ultimate New Heaven and Earth commence their endless dominion. The dispute is over whether the Second Coming of Christ to judge the world occurs before or after the millennium. The difference has come virtually to symbolize the distinction between more sanguine, progressivist views of future history held by liberal Christians – post-millennialism. The more apocalyptic pre-millennialist position of many Fundamentalists relates that times are likely only to get worse until the sudden breakthrough of the *parousia*, the Last Day scenario, of which the millennial reign of Christ is only a follow-up.

Behind these stances lie two radically different views of the relation of Christianity to the world. The same two strands can be found in virtually all religions: the liberal, and what for want of a better word may be called (since conservative is not exactly right, as will be shown) in Christianity, evangelical, and is now more broadly termed fundamentalist.

The liberal position generally urges that the religion be interpreted in terms of the best science, philosophy, historical scholarship, and political currents of the times, as defined by the most eminent secular authorities and opinion-makers. Liberalism is quite willing to subordinate the literal reading of scripture and traditional doctrine, for example, to acceptance of evolution, belief in human progress, even the tenet that miracles do not really happen, in favor of what is seen as the essential moral and spiritual values of the faith behind the symbols. Of such a progressivist, modern view of history as moving always toward greater knowledge, greater fulfillment in human life, post-millennialism is an apt metaphor if taken to delineate a coming golden age climaxed by encounter with God himself, in the spirit of concluding lines from Alfred Lord Tennyson's *In Memoriam*:

> Of those that, eye to eye, shall look
>   On knowledge; under whose command
>   Is Earth and Earth's, and their hand
> Is Nature like an open book;
>
> No longer half-akin to brute,
>   For all we thought and loved and did,
>   And hoped, and suffer'd, is but seed
> Of what in them is flower and fruit . . .
>
> That God, which ever lives and loves,
>   One God, one law, one element,
>   And one far-off divine event,
> To which the whole creation moves.[135]

But the Christian evangelical, and the fundamentalist generally, contends that the religion must always speak in its own language, rather than that of the culture. It thus represents a worldview, and even a universe of discourse, at odds with the prevailing culture, and which could certainly be seen as pronouncing judgment upon it. Like Jesus, it may say that the culture's prestigious spokespersons are whited sepulchers, hypocrites and sinners within, and of their vaunted temples that soon not one stone will be left standing upon another. So it is that this kind of Christian apocalypticism shares the world-stage with the Hindu kaliyuga when only Vishnu returning in the form of Kalki on his white horse can save those still capable of being saved, or the Buddhist Decline of the Dharma toward a time when spirituality has so failed that only bare faith can save, or the Islamic terrible tribulation of the Last Days, when al-Dajjal, the Deceiver, appears.

No secret how these grim but dramatic scenarios at once give the lie to self-satisfied secular thought, with its confident assumptions about the progress being wrought by science, technology, and human schemes for social reform, and offer more than adequate compensation to those who feel something is missing, or something leaves them out, in those brave new worlds. The fact that the Day is soon – could happen tomorrow, or even later today – is no small part of how it one-ups the world with all its complacent plans. This is no 'far-off divine event,' but sudden, as a thief in the night, in the midst of our eating and drinking, marrying and giving in marriage, as in the days of

Noah: 'Then two men will be in the field, one is taken and one is left. Two women will be grinding at the mill; one is taken and one is left. Watch therefore, for you do not know on what day your Lord is coming' (Matt. 24: 38–43).

Eastern Doors to the Apocalypse

According to accepted Pali texts, the nadir of the world as we know it will come some five thousand years after the historical Buddha's entry into Nirvana – that is, around 4456 C.E. Then the Buddha's Dharma will be forgotten, humans will have short and evil lives, all will seem dark indeed. But morning begins at midnight, and in those dismal years the bodhisattva Maitreya, the coming Buddha of the future, will quietly enter the world and the cycle will commence its slow ascent. Finally, after several thousand more years, Earth will be nearly a paradise, with wish-fulfilling trees yielding fruit and long-lived people contented in their happy lot. A *Charkavartin*, or righteous king, will appear to protect the good from what ill still remains through the rule of just law. After him, his way paved by the sublime monarch, Maitreya will be revealed as a full Buddha, ready to turn the wheel of Dharma. Two paths toward perfection then present themselves: the way of right deeds in this world, the way of the Charkravartin; and the way of world-renunciation, the way of the Buddha.[136]

In Thailand today, the Phra Dhammakaya movement represents a comparable form of Buddhist apocalyptic and radical dualism. It views the world as in a crucial, 'end-time' battle between the white or good Dhammakaya (body of the Buddha or Dharma) and the black Dhammakaya or evil Buddha, also identified with Mara, the Buddha's tempter. The black Buddha has nearly driven out his white counterpart and enslaved the world without our even knowing it, in a manner some up-to-date followers have compared to the situation in the film *The Matrix*. The movement exerts all its efforts to help people see through the delusion, and lend energy to the forces of good through meditation.[137]

In China, the White Lotus Society has often carried the banner of Buddhist apocalyptic. Of Manichaean[138] and Maitreyan (related to Maitreya, the coming Buddha of the future) Buddhist background, White Lotus adherents generally believed that the present age, the age of Sakyamuni Buddha, would be succeeded by an imminent future age of Maitreya. The White Lotus was characterized by belief in Wusheng

Iaomu, the Eternal Mother, the ultimate ancestress of the human race, who yearned to rescue those of her children who repented from the evil incumbent to humanity, and deliver them to their true homeland, a paradise of eternal peace and prosperity.[139]

But to get there, a page in the book of world-ages has to be turned. The age coming next ends in paradise, but first its terrible yet hopeful advent sets in motion an apocalyptic scouring of the world to remove all its deeply embedded evil by means of floods, plagues, earthquakes, and other immense catastrophes. By means of such horrendous birth-pangs the planet is torn apart, and the righteous separated from the condemned. Finally, amidst these calamities, at the right hour Maitreya appears as messenger of the Eternal Mother. He delivers her faithful progeny to her, a new and perfect world is created for them out of the ruins of the old, and they enter into it looking forward to an immortality of harmony, justice, and fulfillment.[140]

White Lotus preachers presented themselves as emissaries of the Eternal Mother, not priests of the established religions. The imperial authorities normally looked on these sectarians with suspicion, for the very idea of a better society seemed judgmental toward the present order; the Maitreyans' characteristic emphasis on equality in the coming age appeared subversive of the hierarchical Confucian structure of the present one. And, indeed, from time to time rebellions among the discontented did arise under the White Lotus banner, sometimes under leaders professing to be incarnations of Maitreya, claiming that their violence would hasten the end of the present age and usher in the time of auspicious catastrophes heralding the next.

For example, a rebellion rose in 1774 against the Qing dynasty, under a martial arts and herbal medicine expert called Wang Lun who claimed the support of the Eternal Mother. Although many peasants rallied around him, Wang seems to have had no firm political agenda, just spiritual fire, resentment against the prevailing powers, and belief (like that of the famous 'Boxers' of the 1900 'Boxer Rebellion' against foreign influence in China) that his magical powers would stop bullets of opposing troops.[141]

On the other hand, the denominator White Lotus Society was, according to some authorities, used almost generically by the imperial government to cover a number of rebellious millenarian movements, although the term certainly had a core doctrine and identity of its own.[142] Nancy Chen points out that while White Lotus groups were often quite localized and piecemeal, they did serve as support groups for believers traveling long distances, and the fragments could be aroused and forgathered when occasion summoned.[143] On the other hand, it is true that a wide range of rebellious sectarian movements down to recent times were more or less in the White Lotus lineage: the Red Scarf Society, the Eight Trigram Society, and the already-mentioned 'Boxers' (or 'Righteous and Harmonious Fists') of 1900.[144]

But the most successful millenarian rebellion in China was, surprisingly, not Buddhist, Taoist, or White Lotus, but Christian in inspiration, though having distinctive Chinese features. That was the Taiping rebellion of 1850–1864. It was led by Hong Xiuquan (1813–1864), a troubled young man who, after failing the Confucian examination for civil service advancement, turned to Christianity. Although he had read some Christian literature provided by a missionary, his knowledge of the western faith was far from perfect; he created his own ingenious mix of Christian eschatology and traditional Chinese beliefs. He called his movement Taiping Tiangua – 'Highest Peace Kingdom of God,' the former a term used by various native millenarian rebels throughout Chinese history, the Kingdom of God of course Christian language.

Claiming a vision had revealed to him that he was the second son of God and younger brother of Jesus, Hong then set about to establish God's kingdom on earth in the China of his own day. Capitalizing on widespread discontent with the sclerotic (and not truly Chinese) Manchu dynasty then in power, and with the often-corrupt Confucian meritocracy of mandarins who administered it, the young messianic leader harshly denounced them and proclaimed a new theocratic order based on the equality of all, both men and women, expressed in such practical applications as the redistribution of land with no distinction as to rank or gender, and with preference for communal rather than private ownership. The movement further enjoined education (Christian in character) and adherence to Hong's version of the Ten Commandments. His 'God Worshipers Society' forbade ancestor-worship, the worship of Buddhas and traditional gods, opium, foot-binding, prostitution, and slavery.

Fired by Hong's promise of heavenly life in exchange for earthly martyrdom, organized as an army of God, Taiping forces at first fought successfully against government troops. The religious rebels took Nanjing in 1853, a city Hong identified with the Heavenly Jerusalem of the Book of Revelation and made the capital of his growing empire. For some years the Taiping controlled vast reaches of central China. But as time went on the movement fractured, the traditional regime re-formed and strengthened itself against the challengers, and the western powers – preferring to deal with the worldly Manchu than their over-zealous and heterodox co-religionists – increasingly gave their support to Beijing. The Taiping collapsed in 1864; Hong committed suicide that year just as victorious government forces neared Nanjing. But the Taiping were not forgotten, and undoubtedly provided inspiration for the later, more successful political revolutions of Sun Yat-sen and of the Communists who triumphed in 1949, though the Christian millennialist side of the Taiping was not revived.

The religious aspect of this remarkable rebellion must not be mini-mized, however. A recent study by Thomas H. Reilly has emphasized that Hong's challenge to the emperor was as much or more religious as political; the Taiping leader claimed that the sovereign had usurped the Mandate of Heaven idea so basic to Chinese institutions. Hong signaled that the divine mandate belonged to his movement instead when he called its rule the Kingdom of God. He attacked the traditional city gods and mandarins first wherever his minions went, undermining their conventional support for the old ways. At the same time, by adapting the millennial vision of movements such as the White Lotus as well as the imperial ideology, like every successful reformer he maintained just enough of the old to legitimate the new.[145]

Apocalypse Over and Over

Turning to cyclical views of time and eternity, we might first emphasize that many peoples do not hold a 'steady state' view of time, even after creation, but one that conceives of the creation and destruction of the world to be an ever-repeated event, often catastrophic. The Aztec calendar, for example, as recorded on the famous Sun Stone, depicted Tonatiuh, the sun god, a flint knife for a tongue, demanding the sacrifice of human hearts to keep the world going. Already four cycles of creation and destruction have passed, each commenced with sacrifice by the gods: the jaguar, wind, rain, and water eras, and we are now in the fifth, the 'movement' era, but its continuation depends on bloody hearts offered the sun god, and when its time has passed this era too is bound to come to an end and make way for the next.

The Hindu system, as developed in such texts as the Kūrma Purana, presents four recurring ages. The first, the Krtayuga, was a golden age of bliss, meditation, abundance, and lack of self-interest; the second, the Tretayuga, saw the first arising of personal pleasure and greed; in the third, the Dvaparayuga, incipient lack of self-control led to the clamor of war and the moans of the suffering and dying; in the fourth, the present Kaliyuga, the final effects of this deterioration become all too apparent in shortness of life, hunger, moral decay, and social chaos. All that can be said for the later eras is that means of liberation arise in them; indeed the Kūrma Purana tells us that in the Kali age one can receive merit easily, simply by worshiping God; knowledge of scripture or yoga is not required.[146] At the very end of this last age the final avatar of Vishnu, Kalki, arrives to save those who still can be saved. Otherwise, the cosmos disintegrates into the elements until it is time to begin the cycles again.

The ancient Greeks also had four ages, first declared in Hesiod: Golden, Silver, Bronze, and Iron, though in Hesiod they are really five, since he interposed an age of heroes – the great figures of myth and the Trojan War, now dwelling in the Isles of the Blest – between Bronze and Iron. The last era, after the heroes have departed, our Iron age, is characterized by people like us, worn down and full of care, only enduring till the cycle starts again.[147]

The Golden Age, like visions of the Elysian Fields, evokes images of an earthly paradise that might be accessible, or capable of being built, here and now. While earthly utopias are not, of course, myths of the afterlife, they are worth just a few lines here because their secularization of heaven or the millennium demonstrates the pervasiveness of the dream whether part of a religious worldview or not. The psychological and political dynamics of even the most secular utopia often has theological parallels.

That vision has been mounted in numerous utopias ancient and modern, from Epicurus' appealing garden retreats from the brutality of the Roman world, fellowships warmed by friendship, wine, and Mediterranean sun, to early modern imaginings such as Thomas More's *Utopia* (1516) and Francis Bacon's *New Atlantis* (c. 1623). Under the aegis of the idea of progress, and sometimes associated with Spiritualism, nineteenth-century pictures of the perfect society were enacted by Shakers and Fourierists, or in communities such as Amana, Oneida, or New Harmony. They also took shape in such literary projections as Samuel Butler's *Erewhon* (1872), Edward Bellamy's *Looking Backward: 2000–1887* (1888), and William Morris' *News from Nowhere* (1890). The twentieth century read H. G. Wells, *A Modern Utopia* (1905) and B. F. Skinner's *Walden Two* (1948), as well as 'dystopias,' inspired in large part by skeptical reaction to sanguine fantasies of a new wonder-world made by science and social engineering. Dystopian masterworks are Aldous Huxley's *Brave New World* (1932) and

George Orwell's *Nineteen Eighty-Four* (1948). This is not to mention the innumerable utopias and dystopias created by the burgeoning science fiction literature of the century, or the writings of such important political movements as communism and socialism.

Common features of modern-day Golden Age societies are equality and freedom, together with central planning in order to make the society work, and finally some perhaps draconian means by which human nature is conditioned or adapted to the requirements of such a just, but far from individualistic, society. (Needless to say, utopias generally experience tension between the first two of those desiderata, equality and freedom, and the last two, planning and conditioning; not a few experimental ideal communities have floundered because of individuals more interested in creative freedom than in hard work, or in submission to the Plans.)

As for adapting the old Adam to the new Eden, readers of such dystopian literature as the works of Huxley and Orwell will recall harsh 'conditioning,' including the use of electric shock treatment in *Brave New World*, and the 'Newspeak' of *Nineteen Eighty-Four*, language designed to make it impossible to phrase, or even to think, nonconformist ideas.

Serious utopians, however, believe that some more benign conditioning is compatible with true freedom, just as Christian and other believers hold that living under the guidance of God's grace is perfect freedom. In his novelistic *Walden Two*, the behaviorist psychologist B. F. Skinner seems to me to echo the Protestant experience of sovereign grace as he makes a utopian spokesperson says, '[Through positive reinforcement] we can achieve a sort of control under which the controlled, though they are following a code much more scrupulously than was ever the case under the old system, nevertheless *feel free*. They are doing what they want to do, not what they are forced to do . . . By a careful cultural design, we control not the final behavior, but the *inclination* to behave – the motives, the desires, the wishes. The curious thing is that in that case *the question of freedom never arises*.'[148]

Grace leads to Heaven through whatever suffering, even martyrdom, is required on earth; Utopia makes for Heaven on earth, or so it dreams.

Eternal Recurrence

Another vision which should be mentioned, as a sort of compromise between cyclic and eternal now, is the concept of Eternal Recurrence.

Although it has classical and Indian antecedents, in the notions of the Great Year and the four successive ages already presented, in its modern form Eternal Recurrence is chiefly associated with the philosopher Friedrich Nietzsche. The basic premise is that, if the cosmos contains only a finite amount of matter but time is infinite, the universe having no starting or ending point but is constantly changing, then eventually – over unimaginably long expanses of time – each of its states would recur, not once but an infinite number of times. What you are now doing, and your entire life, has happened not once but over and over beyond measure, and will again innumerable times in the endless future.

Nietzsche never exactly said that believed this stupendous doctrine literally, nor did he deny it; rather, he used it as a touchstone of his philosophy of meaning. He asks the reader in *The Gay Science* how she would feel if some demon were to tell her, 'This life as you now live it and have lived it, you will have to live once more and innumerable times more; and there will be nothing new in it, but every pain and every joy and every thought and sigh and everything unutterably small or great in your life will have to return to you, all in the same succession and sequence . . . The eternal hourglass of existence is turned upside down again and again, and you with it, speck of dust!'[149]

Would you throw yourself down in despair at this ghastly fate, the philosopher asks, or would you, in a glorious upsurge of rapture, reply, 'You are a god and never have I heard anything more divine.' Are you well enough disposed to life 'to crave nothing more fervently than this ultimate eternal confirmation and seal?'[150]

Paradoxically, Eternal Recurrence is at once extreme nihilism – nothing, no life or historical process, finally achieves anything since all will be dissolved in the end only to recur over and over – and yet is also extreme affirmation of life, for it challenges one to believe every moment of life, just as it is, to be literally eternal and so worth ultimate joy. This joy is a consequence of Nietzsche's famous declaration of the Death of God – itself, of course, an eternally recurring death if eternal recurrence is true – for it moves the locus of religious faith from God Above to the timeless moment. 'It is only after the death of religion,' Nietzsche wrote, 'that the invention of the domain of the divine . . . will once again proliferate,' to become 'the religion of religion,' a faith focused on the affirmation of all life and every moment, eternally recurring.[151]

Nietzsche's paradoxical eternity leads us to a further consideration: is eternal life individual, or does it entail absorption of the individual into God?

The One and the Many: Non-Dualism

The problem of oneness versus separateness has spread across the religious world. Of course, in Buddhism ultimate entry into Nirvana, or liberation from name and form through God-realization in Hinduism, means transcending separateness. On the other hand, in monotheistic religion the orthodox view always held that the Creator had to maintain some separateness from the creature, hence total absorption was not possible, though mystics always tended to press as close as imaginable to that ultimate goal in their realization of inner oneness with God, an eternal unitive state. At present we will look at this paradox chiefly through examples from the Hindu tradition, where it is vividly and graphically portrayed in the twin paths of non-dualism, the Advaita Vedanta of the great philosopher Shankara, and in Bhakti, the way of love.

For Shankara, advocating the philosophy of Advaita Vedanta or non-dualism, exponent of the way of jñana or wisdom more than of love, once fully realized the seer could have no separate existence, for it and all its world are but maya, illusion. It would seem that then Krishna and all his revels ought to fade away like mists when the sun has risen, and that even the noblest afterlife would involve fantasies of separateness. Shankara said:

> Cease to identify yourself mistakenly with all those coverings, such as the ego, etc., which overlie the Atman. Brahman alone remains – supreme, infinite, changeless, the one without a second ... The world of appearances is a mere phantom; there is but one Reality. It is changeless, formless and absolute ... Into it the causes of our delusion melt away, as darkness melts into light ... The universe no longer exists after we have awakened into the highest consciousness in the eternal Atman, which is Brahman, devoid of any distinction or division.[152]

Even so, it appears that the subtle meanings of mystic union can also be expressed in myth-like story, though there are those who have claimed that Advaita or non-dualism is a 'myth-buster,' showing the inadequacy of all mythic interpretations of ultimate religious truth.

It is rather in the realm of karmic reincarnation or rebirth that myth could have a place, as part of the avidya or 'not seeing,' of dwelling in the mayavic hall of mirrors. Shankara was thus willing to use language at least story-like to describe that side of things:

> I have entered this body as a bird enters a nest, by force of the merit and demerit accumulated by myself. Again and again by force of the merit and demerit, when this body perishes, I shall enter another body as a bird enters another nest when its previous one has been destroyed. Thus I am in beginningless transmigratory existence. I have been abandoning (old) bodies which have been obtained one after another in the spheres of gods, animals, men, and hells by force of my own *karman* and I have been getting other new bodies over and over again. I am forced by my own *karman* to rotate in the incessant cycle of birth and death as in the waterwheel . . .[153]

But is myth inadequate or just another kind of language? Madhusudana Sarasvati (sixteenth to seventeenth centuries), a highly regarded exponent of Advaita Vedanta, was also a fervent devotee of Krishna. For Madhusudana, the god of love and play was an avatar or embodiment not only of Saguna Brahman (Brahman 'with attributes,' that is, ultimate reality as it manifests in the face and form of the gods or, for advaitins, as we humans 'superimpose' face and form on God, as accommodations to our limitations), but even of Nirguna Brahman (Brahman 'without attributes,' in his absolute nature), for Krishna is, paradoxically, the personification of 'the nondual Self, a mass of perfect Being, Consciousness, and Bliss, the pure Existence which is the substratum of all . . . Beyond Krishna, I do not know of any higher reality.'[154]

The eminent indologist Heinrich Zimmer once wrote, undoubtedly with Advaita Vedanta in mind:

> Indian symbols of art voice the same truth as Indian philosophy and myth. They are signals along the way of the same pilgrim's progress, directing human energies to the same goal of transmutation. Our task, then, as students of Indian myth and symbol, is to understand the abstract conceptions of India's philosophical doctrines as a kind of intellectual commentary on what stands crystallized and unfolded in the figures and patterns of symbols and art, and, conversely, to read the symbols as the pictorial script of India's ultimately changeless wisdom.[155]

And now, more about Krishna and other moving symbols of the changeless wisdom.

The One and the Many: Bhakti

Bhakti or devotional love, the great stream of Hinduism moving toward oneness with God, rejects unconditioned absorption into Brahman because love always requires the other – the beloved to whom the lover wants always to draw closer and closer. Yet the distinction could never be totally abolished, for then where would the love go? (Indeed, the word bhakti comes from bhai, 'two,' the same Indo-European root found in such words as bicycle, bisect, etc.) The great mystery of love is that it wants always to be one, yet must always be two, and in that very conundrum is its delight. In human love one can grow extremely close, so that a parent can virtually know what her child is thinking, or a lover his beloved, yet love also is greatly aware of the two ness, knowing well that the beloved is an Other as well as a Self.

Bhakti says take this quality of human love and transfer it also to the grandest love of all, that of the soul for the divine. So it is that Jadunath Sinha, interpreting the great ancient sage of bhakti, Narada, profoundly commented,

> Then the devotee consecrates his whole being to the beloved, loses himself in Him, and feels His living presence everywhere. And, finally, he feels the pang of separation from his Beloved, which is the highest consummation of love. Union is tinged with selfishness. Separation is selfless. Even in separation higher union is felt. The devotee is eternally united with Him in his separation from Him.[156]

For Ramanuja and other modified non-dualist theologians of bhakti, this oneness in separateness is carried over into the afterlife as well. Individual souls abide in Brahman, sharing in his being and bliss, but not all his infinite knowledge nor his ultimate creativity. Yet Ramanuja is able to describe Vishnu, as the supreme divine form, in highly personal/mythological language:

> He who is always gloriously visible is the pre-eminent Person who dwells within the orb of the sun. His splendor is like that of a colossal mountain of molten gold and His brilliance that of the rays of hundreds of thousands of suns. His long eyes are spotless like the

petals of a lotus that, sprouting forth from deep water on a soft stalk, blossoms in the rays of the sun. His eyes and His forehead and His nose are beautiful, His coral-like lips smile graciously, and His soft cheeks are beaming . . . He looks upon the hosts of His devotees with loving eyes, filled with compassion and affection. His sport is to evolve, sustain and dissolves all the worlds. All evil is foreign to Him – He is the treasury of all beautiful qualities and He is essentially different from all other entities.[157]

On the devotional approach, here are some lines from the account of the love between Krishna and the Gopi or shepherdesses (more literally, cowgirls or milkmaids). Krishna is sometimes seen as the most beloved avatar or incarnation of Vishnu, sometimes as himself supreme Godhead. In any case, the playful love shared by the god and his dearest devotees is taken by bhaktas as emblematic of the love between God and the souls of his devotees:

Sri Krishna is the embodiment of love. Love is divine, and is expressed in many forms. To Yasoda [his mother], the God of Love was her own baby Krishna; to the shepherd boys, Krishna was their beloved friend and playmate; and to the shepherd girls, Krishna was their beloved friend, lover, and companion.

When Sri Krishna played on his flute, the shepherd girls [milkmaids] forgot everything; unconscious even of their own bodies, they ran to him, drawn by his great love . . .

Krishna, who gives delight to all and who is blissful in his own being, divided himself into as many Krishnas as there were shepherd girls, and danced and played with them. Each girl felt the divine presence and divine love of Sri Krishna. Each felt herself the most blessed. Each one's love for Sri Krishna was so absorbing that she felt herself one with Krishna – nay, knew herself to be Krishna.[158]

It is said in the Srimad Bhagavata Purana that when Krishna played his flute, the music aroused Kama, the god of erotic feeling, leading the milkmaids to abandon all and follow him. On hearing those irresistible notes, those who were milking left off before finishing, or let milk on the stove boil over, or neglecting their eating or dressing ran to meet their divine Lord in disarray. Even husbands and babies were forfeited for a more compelling love; the sounds of Krishna's flute are essentially anarchic, disruptive of all ordinary hierarchy and social order, for duty and family were nothing to the bhaktas' love for the comely, playful, and provocative young god. Krishna 'played softly, capturing the hearts of the beautiful-eyed women . . . their hearts had been stolen by Govinda [Krishna], so they did not turn back when their husbands, fathers, brothers, and relatives tried to prevent them. They were in a state of rapture.'[159]

They were called to *lila*, divine play, play without purpose outside itself, play like that of Krishna or God himself when he made the world, for God did not *need* the world, being complete as he was, but wanted to create just as one wants to dance or frolic, to play a game or just play for the sake of playing. To follow Krishna in his revels is like returning to this state of ideal childlikeness, as on the best days of remembered childhood, to that state of primal creative freedom yet also or ultimate wisdom.

This took place in the lush gardens of Vrindaban, a city still sacred to Lord Krishna, idealized in art and verse as, in Krishna's time, a place of superlative sensuous appeal, of flowers and fragrances in the air and soft breezes: everything to enhance the passionate but pure love of God and the Gopis, who represent the souls of all who love God, or strive to do so.

Nor was that all. For Krishna devotionalism teaches that when the God of Love returned to his heavenly abode, he took with him these gardens and their inflamed devotees, to become an eternal Vrindaban, where the Gopis forever pursue their immortal lover, and he unceasingly dances with each separately, as though she were his alone.

Moreover, it is said that all true worshipers of Krishna down to the present may be reborn in the Heavenly Vrindaban. From this paradise there is no earthly rebirth or reincarnation, for devotional love burns away all karma and attachment, so releases one from incarnation again in this world. But in the Heavenly Vrindaban, even if one is not quite worthy of rebirth there as a Gopi, it would be enough just become a single flower in the soil of that blessed land, which might be touched by the deity's dancing feet, or a bird forever signing his praises. Here surely is a myth of the afterlife worthy of the oneness-in-separateness attained by love, rather than the more literal oneness of sheer monistic union. David R. Kinsley has written of Krishna:

He is the embodiment of all that is implied in the word *lila*: light, almost aerial activity, boisterous revelry, frivolity, spontaneity, and freedom.

In Vrindaban Krishna's life is a continuous song, a melodious, harmonious symphony of beauty, grace, and joy. Here God plays,

losing himself in ecstatic, spontaneous revelry. Here life is a celebration, not a duty. Here life does not grind along but scampers
in dance and rejoices in song. All that makes life in the pragmatic
world endurable is to be found here. This is the other world of the
divine, from which beauty, freedom, and bounty proceed. Here the
bondage of necessity does not exist. Krishna is here, filling the world
with the melody of his flute. And those who have heard it say:
'Without Krishna there is no song.'[160]

The Bird of Oneness and Manyness

Consider also the Simorgh. This giant but benevolent bird is a common figure in Iranian mythology, similar to the Roc in the Arabian
Nights and other Arab folklore. Large enough to carry off an elephant,
and brilliant as a peacock, sometimes bearing a human face, this
avian was compassionate and female. Some said that like the phoenix,
she lived a very long life, then renewed herself out of the flames
of her destruction. The Simorgh, who favored high mountains for
her dwelling, was believed to purify surrounding land and bestow
fertility.

The kindly nature of the Simorgh is exhibited in a story from the
epic *Shahname* (Book of Kings), a vivid narrative of ancient Iranian
rulers written by the poet Ferdowsi about 1000 C.E. According to it, a
certain Prince Zal, son of King Saam, was born albino; the supersti-
tious ruler assumed he was the son of a devil, and had him abandoned
on a mountaintop. But the Simorgh, whose dwelling place it was,
heard the child's piteous cries, and took the prince to raise as her own
son. She taught him much wisdom, and when he finally felt he had to
return to the world of men, gave him three feathers to burn if he
needed help. That time came when his beautiful wife Rudaba was in a
very difficult labor and near death; the Simorgh was summoned, and
taught Zal how to save her and the infant through a caesarian section;
the newborn in time became the great hero Rostam.

More relevant to our purpose, though, is the way in which the
Sirmorgh became a metaphor for God in the literature of Sufism or
mystical Islam. The most famous example is the book of poems by
Farid ud-Din Attar called *The Conference of the Birds* (1177). In it, a
large group of birds, representing disciples, are led by the hoopoe, an
impressive old-world bird with a fanlike crest. That avian mentor is
allegorically a Sufi *sheikh*, or spiritual master, and he is guiding his

docents on a journey to find the Simorgh – a venture emblematic of the quest for enlightenment.

On the difficult trip they pass through seven valleys indicating seven stations of the spiritual life such as love, gnosis, detachment, seeing the unity of God, bewilderment, and finally selflessness and *fana*, or falling into self-forgetfulness in God. Nearly all give up, leaving only thirty birds (the word Simorgh can also mean thirty birds in Persian) who arrive at the land of the Simorgh.

But there they see no gigantic, brilliantly colored bird – only a lake in which the images of the thirty successful questers are reflected. The lesson they must learn is that God is not something huge and other than themselves, but simply their own being. God, in Sufi doctrine, is not external or separate from the universe, but is the underlying totality of all being, in the birds, the lake, and all that is.

The wise teacher, having taken this reflective guise, says:

> I am a mirror set before your eyes,
> And all who come before my splendour see
> Themselves, their own unique reality . . .
> Though you have struggled, wandered, travelled far,
> It is yourself you see and what you are . . .
> You find in me the selves you were before.[161]

To be sure, the ultra-orthodox criticized Attar's verse for suggesting pantheism, but by putting his message in quasi-mythical form he avoids dogmatic statements, leaving the reader with a sense of what the recognition of ultimate divine oneness means to the experiencer. Whatever God is, she or he is none other than my own true nature, known when I truly know myself.

Chapter 10

Common and Uncommon Faith:
The Afterlife in Folk Religion and the
Great Tradition

Parallel Worlds

Folklorists have often pointed to Russia as a country where folk religion and Eastern Orthodox Christianity have coexisted as virtually parallel cultures, a situation Russians call *dvoeverie*, or two faiths. One is Christian, the other pagan in origin. The pagan wing is based on the earth mother, the world tree, shamanistic wisdom, and innumerable spirits of places like the bath and the attic. We can here only look at examples of Russian folk religion related to the afterlife.

Birds, considered to be messengers between this life and the other world, have a special role in this folklore. Their songs and cries, if they could be understood as they are by the wise, are foretellings of what is to come, including death. Tuvan Siberians, for example, say that the call of a horned owl near a house forebodes the death of a child, even as the black woodpecker forecasts weather. In Russia the egg is not only a symbol of new life, as is the Easter egg in many cultures, but also links death and life. At an ancient, probably pre-Christian, festival of the dead called Radunitsa, people come together in cemeteries to picnic with the departed, and to leave eggs as gifts for their ancestors. As they leave them, they ritually lament, yet depart in hope for newness of life.[162]

Such parallel or layered culture is hardly limited to mystic Russia. In Southeast Asia austere Theravada Buddhism shares spiritual space with popular culti of nature spirits, *nats* in Burma and *phis* in Thailand. Until the forced separation of Shinto and Buddhism in Japan in the nineteenth century, the Shinto kami (deities) resided in shrines beside great Buddhist temples, where they were considered guardians of the Buddhas, students of their dharma, or even the same lines of spiritual power in native Japanese rather than Buddhist garb. Nor are parallel spiritual cultures limited to 'exotic' Asian or peasant cultures.

I recall that many years ago, as a very young clergyman in rural middle America, gradually learning that not only was there formal church religion, but also private talk of such cosmic religion-type matters as plowing by the phases of the moon, near-death experiences, healing springs related to Native Americans, UFO sightings, and on a more literary plane, belief in reincarnation and the like fostered by reading of Theosophical and Vedanta Society books available in the local public library. At the least, these perceptions helped give people a sense of power over health and destiny outside the hierarchies of medical, religious, and educational professionals on which moderns can so often feel too dependent. To boot, the possibility of flying saucers or spirits of the dead visiting our flat cornfields of a quiet evening added a sense of wonder to hardscrabble lives, infusing them with ways to move into closer harmony with the cycles of nature.

Most societies actually have two faiths, like traditional Russia. Consider the distinction between the Great and Little Traditions of religions, terms used by the anthropologist Robert Redfield.[163] The Great Tradition is that version of the faith taught in major universities and divinity schools. It is usually in dialogue with current science, social science, and philosophy; its learning is in a lineage with that of the culture's long past and its historical awareness.

The Great Tradition version of a major religion is highly literate, engaged in exegetical scriptural study, creedal definitions, ecclesiastical councils, and ventures into philosophical theology. The great majority of the world's faiths today, as we have seen, are grounded in the Axial Age transformation of religion by the acts and legacy of a Founder. So it is that historical placement of the creed and its development down the centuries that are central to Great Tradition consciousness.

The Great Tradition unpacks as far as possible the Axial Age religions' *nature* as faiths based on remembered historical moments, moments which birthed scriptures, doctrines, liturgies, and institutional structures capable of export around the globe. It talks about the faith in measured language, takes the long view, values institutional stability, promotes sympathetic education, sees itself represented in the classic art of the culture it governs, loves to embody itself in splendid architecture and dramatic ritual or homiletic. The Great Tradition tends to emphasize the historical rather than cosmic aspects of the faith, to prefer intellectual sophistication to unbridled feeling, to mistrust charismatic personalities, and to value interaction with the society's 'mainstream' cultural, political, economic, educational, and social life.

The Little Tradition

That kind of awareness contrasts with the Little Tradition or folk religion version, where consciousness of religious reality is far more ahistorical, formatted in story or iconic phrase and representation, even non-verbal. This other expression is the popular or folk version of the same faith, no doubt well intermixed with items from previous, especially cosmic, religious ways of dealing with the world and human life. Its main imperative is to make religion compatible not so much with academic science and philosophy, as with the 'best' of everyday *personal* life, in interaction with the physical self, family, community, and nature, and equally with one's capacity of for dream and imagination.

The Little Tradition is religion as it understood locally, and conveyed by myth or scripture received uncritically, as a kind of talisman. Because of its lack of effective historical perspective, Little Tradition after the Axial Age will be essentially a cosmic religion version of the Founder religion. This is, for example, the popular and folk Christianity wherein Christmas and Easter are seasonal festivals of solstice and spring, days of wonder more than historical commemorations. Replete with cosmic and fertility symbols from world-tree and lights to flowers, eggs, and rabbits, they recall magical events which occurred in a mythic 'other time,' an 'age of miracles,' different in nature from the everyday present, but which point to season and celebration in that present. The same may be said for Passover, the Hindu Holi (associated with fertility and the god Krishna), and the commemoration of the Buddha's birth, enlightenment, and entry into Nirvana called Vesak or, in Japanese, Hanamatsuri ('flower festival'), all like Easter spring festivals aligned with the full moon.

Regarding the afterlife, the Great Tradition in modern times is likely to philosophize it into a matter of timeless states of consciousness and the presence of the divine, in somewhat the way of Platonic or Vedanta thought. The Little Tradition afterlife will usually be more personal, like our everyday self-awareness, oriented to particular places as though heaven and hell were distant extensions of the gardens and garbage dumps of this world, and to think in terms of long journeys, perhaps heralded or guided by saints, angels, or birds.

In connection with life after death, folk or popular religion generally has much more continuity with cosmic religion than the history-oriented and text-oriented versions of the great tradition. It is also likely that after-death fate looms larger as the real purpose of religion on the popular level than for the elites. The Little Tradition is commonly known as folk religion in premodern societies where it is largely based on peasant culture, and as popular religion in modern societies where it is practiced by perhaps superficially literate ordinary people.

Some very popular festivals in America and elsewhere, like Halloween, significantly associated with the dead and their spirits, are even more purely pre-Christian cosmic religion in background, though tenuously validated as the eve of All Saints Day, November 1. Their vitality shows the enduring power of that background. Grey Gundaker, in 'Halloween Imagery in Two Southern Settings,' describes poignantly a combination Halloween and birthday party for a dead three-month-old child she observed set up at his tomb in a cemetery, complete with quasi-humorous skeletons and ghosts placed around the infant's grave.[164]

Little Tradition religion is basically transmitted through family, community, and charismatic figures such as shamans, 'holy men,' popular evangelists (today on television more than on the sawdust trail), and wise women, as well as through the local clerical representatives of the Great Tradition. In their villages or the neighborhoods, however, such officiants usually find they do well tacitly to accept as 'implicit faith' the Little Tradition's understanding of the sacred.

So it is that Little Tradition religion centers on seasonal festivals, community folkways, fundamentally on things that are *done* – practices, pilgrimage, preaching, rite – on *feelings* – of divine love, fear, salvation – and on *tangible* sacred objects, from shrines to talismans. It has far less use for the books – except as scripture may become like a talisman – or the rationalized concepts of the Great Tradition.

Popular Images of the Afterlife

We have already surveyed images common to pre-Axial Age cosmic religion. The soul may reside at the place of interment, at an ancestral shrine, or journey far away to a new home in the sky or under the earth.

Or perhaps the seed of life may take temporary root in a dreamland alternative to this world from which return is feasible, or it may cross over to a distant but visible island or mountain on the horizon of our sphere. The intangible remains may even be divided to accomplish these diverse yet desirable missions. Or life may reincarnate, perhaps once again in the same family. The afterlife individual is pictured mentally in human shape, or at least in humanlike angelic form, though that may not always be the case in the Great Tradition. Such images prevail in folk or popular religion now almost as much as ever, even if housed within an Axial Age religion.

The common motif is that in all instances the postmortem destiny is attained immediately, or within a humanly comprehensible span of time. It is not, in other words, conditioned by historical awareness. No last judgment or resurrection of the dead awaits the deceased only after a long progression of years, when the curtain finally rings down on linear, historical duration. Instead, popular and folk religion, like cosmic, is mainly concerned with proper respect for the body, the immediate or near-term destiny of the soul, and the healing of family and community. It is almost as though, on many levels, cosmic religion, not Axial Age religions of history, has won in the end just by persevering and subtly pouring the new wine into old bottles. A glance at death and funerary customs around the religious world may spell out this conclusion more fully.

Chinese Funerals

Perhaps nowhere are funeral customs more elaborate than in China. (The elaborateness of the following is of course dependent on the wealth of the family, and today also the degree of its secularization, but the basic structure obtains.)

Death is anticipated long before the actual event. Elderly people traditionally devote themselves to spiritual preparation; they may even plan their own coffin, and design the garments they are to wear on the last journey. When passing is imminent, the dying person is moved into a special room of the house containing the tablets of the ancestors she or he will soon join, surrounded by relatives. As soon as death occurs, the family members begin wailing and lamenting, sounds which not only express grief but are believed to help collapse barriers the deceased will encounter in the underworld passage. Mourners also remove adornments and put on rough sackcloth, then announce the parting to the outside world through hanging blue and white lanterns, and white banners or strips of paper, at the front door.

A diviner or expert in *feng-shui* (geomancy) is brought in to determine when and in what direction the soul will depart the body, as well as the best time and place for removing the coffin for burial. The body is then ritually washed, dressed in new 'longevity' clothes, and decorated with jade, pearls, coins, and other auspicious valuables, some of which are placed in the mouth, and set up before a kind of temporary altar in the house, where prayers and offerings are made on behalf of the deceased.

For the funeral itself, the body is placed in a heavy black coffin together with cakes to distract the vicious dogs of the underworld, and sealed to the accompaniment of loud wailing. Then follow a complex series of rituals, some in the home with the coffin and some in the temple of the local deity. Taoist priests pray for the soul's admission to paradise, sometimes performing spectacular gymnastics in dramatic enactments of the soul's journey through many obstacles, and their own shaman-like ventures to retrieve the soul from the hells and set it on the right path. The deceased may be represented by a paper figure, moved around as the drama progresses. Often the perils of the underworld journey are theatrically displayed by performers twirling flaming ropes or sticks, as well as tumbling and cartwheels. Finally the decedent soul, now riding a horse and carrying wads of paper money to cover fees, arrives before the dread court of the underworld. His name is read out in an official voice, together with assurances that his papers are in order, his offenses erased by the elaborate funeral performances, and a favorable judgment looks promising.

One more major ordeal remains, however. A mock bridge is placed on the temple stage, a priest disguised as an old man hobbles in. He represents the earth god, who after some comic banter tells how difficult it will be to cross this bridge, beset with monsters and demons, without the help of a god. The deceased's relatives in the audience line up to put money in a bowl until that deity determines it is enough; he then leads the soul to the other side, sliding the paper figure over the bridge as he goes.[165]

At the same time, Buddhist monks perform a series of rituals intended to transfer merit from bodhisattvas and the monks themselves to the dead to cancel out his or her bad karma. Presentations of food, eaten by the living as a kind of communion, are made. Outside the home, offerings in the form of paper homes, clothes, equipment, and great wads of underworld money are burned in order to go with the departed on the great journey, where it will be put to good use.

Finally, when the day assigned by the diviner for burial arrives, a funeral procession is mounted to the cemetery, on a way lit by lanterns. The coffin, carried by pallbearers or, today, often in a vehicle, is accompanied by an empty chair for the deceased to sit in as he or she enjoys the ceremony. The remains are followed by a band and a long train of mourners in rough garments. At last, the coffin is lowered into the grave, abetted by wailing and music. More paper offerings are presented at graveside. Then, in an important ceremony, the senior living member of the family adds a final dot in vermilion ink to the spirit-tablet of the deceased, signifying it is now the soul's official residence. It will be taken back and placed in the same family ceremonial hall in which the soul had left the body.[166]

Recent research indicates that, since the liberalization of the People's Republic of China that started around 1980, traditional religions, including funeral rites, have returned in forms quite similar to what went before. They are somewhat curtailed, so that a ritual that might have then taken three days now may be a day and a half, some official music may be played, and the Taoist and Buddhist temple rituals may be omitted if qualified priests are not available. But traditional hospitality, geomancy, procession, and rites such as feeding hungry ghosts on behalf of the deceased are carried out. Although funerals may still be a family's greatest expense, they are important to its prestige and solidarity; there is also still a sense, however vague, that traditional rituals exert a benign magical influence to the benefit of all.[167]

Clearly, ceremonies like these do not involve the larger philosophical dimensions of Taoism or Buddhism, with belief in the oneness of all or even of the technical non-existence of the soul, though like the Tibetan Book of the Dead these rites presuppose a residual karmic body setting out on a pilgrimage through the various planes of existence. Nor do they much refer to the historical Buddha or Laozi. The Chinese rites are rooted in primal affirmation of the soul, its numinous yet precarious quality, and its cosmological journey. The realm to which it travels is similar to this one, and indeed in a mysterious sense continuous with our world, so that situations there, such as poverty or other misfortune, affect life here, and vice versa. Comparable patterns can be detected in the folk expressions of other historical faiths.

Hinduism

Hindus ideally wish to die by the sacred River Ganges, or at least to have the remains brought to its banks for cremation and the scattering of the ashes in its waters. The funeral pyre is properly lit by the eldest son, who also smashes the skull at the right moment. The ceremony is supervised by a low class of brahmins, who chant ritual verses as the body is consumed by flame and then dispersed. These rites suggest three points of meaning: the body is unimportant of itself, but should be disposed of correctly; fire has a cleansing and recycling function; continuity of the family, as seniority is passed from father to son, is crucial at a time of loss. Although there are other venues where the souls of the departed are prayed for, and where the also-important doctrine of reincarnation is explained, on the burning ghats by the Ganges the even more ancient concepts of cleansing and transition are central.

Judaism

In Judaism, ritual details vary among different wings of the ancient faith. There is no set funeral service, though all prayer books and rabbinic manuals contain acceptable forms. The body is promptly washed, dressed, and prepared for interment. The service generally begins in the home or a funeral parlor, and then is moved to the cemetery for final rites; arrangements are kept simple, without elaborate floral displays or other ornaments. Tradition says that burial should be done as soon as possible after death. But it is customary to pluck a little grass on leaving the burial grounds: 'They of the city shall flourish like the grass of the earth' (Ps. 72:16).

Those lines remind us that the pivotal meaning of this rite, as of any funeral obsequies, involves the importance of this individual to family and community. The loss is deeply mourned, but family and Jewish society must go on. The first week after the death (*shiv'ah*) is observed intensely; relatives stay at home except for the funeral, abstain from washing, wearing shoes, and sexual activity; this is called 'sitting *shiv'ah*.' Friends are expected to visit and console the survivors during this time. They, or the community, provide a meal after return from the cemetery.

A doxology with prayers for the deceased called Kaddish ('Holy [One]' in Aramaic) is said frequently for eleven months at the end of services, properly at the grave by family also, thereafter on the anniversary of the death.[168] The Kaddish of mourners is recited standing, facing Jerusalem, and requires a complement of ten (males in Orthodox Judaism) to be correct.[169]

Islam

In the Islamic world, the Qur'an is read aloud to a dying person. After death, the body is washed and clothed in a seamless white garment, like that worn on the pilgrimage to Mecca, as though in preparation for the last and greatest pilgrimage of all. Burial is done quickly, and the body is placed in the grave facing the holy city. Prayers may be said at the home or in the cemetery. A meal follows. Mourning lasts three days, after which the loss is to be accepted as the will of God and life goes on, though a widow is expected to remain in seclusion four months and ten days, as prescribed in the Qur'an.

Popular death and afterlife beliefs, however, may be less austere than that simple ceremony might suggest. A famous storyteller of the seventh century, Tamin al-Dari, told of angels of death rushing to the dying faithful with balm, basil, and silken garments to lift the soul from the body and carry it to paradise. However, after a brief opportunity to savor the delights of the other world, the spirit is returned to the corpse, often in time for the washing of the body (when its presence can sometimes be sensed), certainly by the time the procession to the grave is completed. At first, angels good and bad war over it, forcing the spirit, if it can, to give the right answers to such questions as, 'What is your religion? Who is your Prophet?' If the answers are satisfactory, the soul of the deceased should be allowed to rest peacefully in the grave – or, according to some folklore, have experiences conditioned by behavior in this life – until the resurrection, when she or he will enter heaven decisively.[170]

All this transpires in a mysterious borderland region, or time, known as *al-barzakh*, a term which more broadly means a barrier, a wall of separation, yet which like any wall also conjoins two sides. Between interment and resurrection one exists on this borderline, except for martyrs, who go straight to paradise. A boundary is always a place of ambiguity, yet also of magic and otherwise forbidden knowledge, for one can see both sides; a saint is sometimes called a *barzakh*.

To be sure, strict philosophers have disputed even the existence of *al-barzakh*, claiming that both soul and body cannot endure without each other, and so both are destroyed at death, to be re-created at the resurrection. But like comparable rigorous ideas in other religions, such logic does not suit the both and needs of folk religion, which as always knows of more things in heaven and earth than are dreamt of in philosophy.[171]

Christian Funerals

Christian funeral customs vary considerably throughout world, often in accordance with local folk culture. Not a great deal is known about early Christian burial, but at first probably followed Roman practice, no doubt with the exclusion of pagan elements and the substitution of more appropriate symbols (such as the Good Shepherd found on early Christian mausolea) and biblical readings. By the fourth century, Christian funerals appear to have consisted of three stages: preparation, processional, and burial, with appropriate prayers, hymns, psalms, and prayer at each stage. The first was washing and clothing the body, in a way suggesting baptism; then the remains were carried in procession to the place of burial, perhaps stopping at the church on the way for prayer, reading of scripture, and a Eucharist. Then, at the graveside, the body was commended to God.[172]

Later popular practices, outside of formal religious services, have ranged from the sometimes bibulous wakes of Irish, Brazilian, and other cultures, and the lively 'jazz funerals' with their powerful cathartic effect in New Orleans, to the other extreme of Victorian British and American mourning. The latter made serious demands, particularly on women of the middle and upper classes.

Women in mourning would wear special heavy, concealing black dresses, including veils of black crepe and caps or bonnets in the same color. Even mourning jewelry was recommended, featuring a 'jet' or polished black stone often embellished with a bit of hair from the deceased, and cameos or lockets bearing his or her picture. Men would wear a very dark suit with black armband, or if in uniform just the armband. These clothes would be worn for varying periods depending on the mourner's closeness to the decedent, for a spouse two years or even longer; Queen Victoria, as is well known, chose to dress in mourning for Prince Albert the rest of her long life, no doubt contributing much to the age's vogue for conspicuous grief. Corresponding black-edged stationery, cards, plaques, and elaborate gravestones were likewise thought suitable. It is no doubt significant that it was the nineteenth century that first (since ancient Egypt) introduced modern embalming and the use of metal rather than wooden caskets, seemingly to deny the reality of physical decay on the part of the corpse.[173]

Today, mourning dress is little regarded, except at the funeral itself, but other customs persist: the procession, the funeral meal, placing flowers periodically at the grave or mausoleum. However varied the practice, all these represent ways of symbolizing that a loss – a severe rupture in one's life – has occurred, that it requires expression in order to heal, that healing must occur for life on this plane to go on. Yet, outside the language of the funeral liturgy itself, little in these patterns can be regarded as distinctively Christian; they are instead pathetically and universally human.

The funeral wake of popular culture is not given over to watching and praying; the mortician's countermanding of fleshly decomposition is hardly the resurrection of the body on the Last Day. The trend in funerals is now toward a festive 'celebration' of the deceased's life for than mourning. Often the service is relatively informal, with participation by many persons who wish to offer a poem, song, or remembrance of the departed one.[174] Cremation is steadily replacing burial. Talk is heard of 'green' funerals and cemeteries, in which ashes are spread, or biodegradable caskets placed, in natural though park-like settings reserved for this purpose, but without ostentatious markers.[175]

Nonetheless, funeral practices old and new clearly answer, in particular cultural terms, to poignant feelings shared by mortals everywhere. The persistent funeral meal continues the universal sense that sharing food has deep communal meaning, bespeaking without words mutual support on profound levels, the nourishing of soul as well as body, the message that family and community continue after the loss of a member even as before. Whether the body is dispatched of by burial or the scattering of ashes, the suggestion is of return to the earth, which is always renewing itself.

Contemporary Popular Images of the Afterlife

A recent poll by the well-regarded Pew Forum on Religion and Public Life found that in 2008, 74% of Americans professed belief in heaven and 59% in hell.[176] As we have seen, a 2005 Harris poll also indicated that 21% of Americans believed in reincarnation; it reported 70% believing in life after death and 70% in heaven, but only 59% in hell.

To be sure, such figures can be quite inaccurate in any scientific sense, owing to the vagueness of much religious belief. Responses are often highly subjective, dependent on the particular way a question is put and the language used (in one poll a notably higher percentage of respondents paradoxically said they believed in heaven than in an afterlife), and perhaps also on the 'ought' factor. (Pollsters have long been aware that in polls regarding religion and moral values, a significant number of respondents will inevitably give the answer they think they 'ought' to give, rather than what, deep down, they really think or what would reflect the way they really live.)

What is clear is that most people who believe in an afterlife at all, or hope there is one (different questions in some polls), most readily affirm a near-term postmortem destination, whether heaven, hell, or reincarnation. (Other theologically possible options, such as purgatory, or oblivion until the general resurrection, are not usually asked.) Informal observation and conversation bears this out. Some talk about passage to the same sort of afterlife presented by the also-popular near-death experience literature: a journey down a tunnel, an encounter with a being of light (sometimes Jesus), and entry into a luminous, paradisaic realm forever – unless one returns, or is reincarnated. Hell may be affirmed on theological grounds, or made the subject of jokes, but does not seem to be treated as a truly live option in most of popular culture.

On the other hand, the war-in-heaven eschatology of works like the 'Left Behind' series and popular evangelicalism is certainly part of this culture too. But it may be noted that apocalyptic scenarios of this sort share the immediacy of cosmic religion rather than the long historical view of Great Tradition Axial Age religion, though they are linked to the revelations of historical founders and scriptures. One might say they are like populist hybrids of cosmic and historical faith. But in their ultimate nature one senses a closer similarity to the prophecies and performances of cosmic-era shamanism than to historical religion.

The time of troubles and apocalyptic sunrise are imminent, expected in our own day. The faithful, like the 'tribulation force' of 'Left Behind' enact the shaman's theatrical role as psychopomp and soul-rescuer. And, as always in folk or popular protests, radical social change yearned for by those who feel themselves disempowered is attained not through difficult political struggle, but through divine intervention abetted by the prayers, demonstrations, heroism, and magic of the faithful. Not only that, but these visions add brilliant notes of miracle and drama to existences that otherwise may seem drab, too routinized by technological civilization, lived by people who feel too out of control of their own lives.

The afterlife of folk and popular religion, then, has points of contact with the Great Tradition, but meets the needs of persons with different mindsets, and different lives, from those of the intellectual and religious establishments.

Chapter 11

Retrospect: Afterlife and Culture

Myths and images of the afterlife could be considered from the perspective of a number of theories about myth. In an earlier book, *Myth: Key Concepts in Religion*,[177] I surveyed several leading academic models for the subject, among them the euhemerist, structuralist, functionalist, psychoanalytic, romantic, and pedagogical. Afterlife affirmations and their subjective reflections could clearly fit into any of these categories.

Briefly, the euhemerist belief that myths are exaggerated tales of ancient kings and heroes could be perceived as the eternal honoring of great kings and heroes now dwelling in the Isles of the Blest, or the equivalent, given that a people makes the assumption that individuals sufficiently great must be undying. Structuralism, with its view that myth is a kind of language through whose grammar polarities are reconciled, could posit in myths and images of the afterlife the reconciliation of some of the profoundest polarities, and attendant anxieties, of this world: life and death, time and timelessness, the often-unpunished evil here below and ultimate retribution. Capping this realm with another makes a whole out of the fragmented half-lives of those here born to sorrow or incompletion. As for functionalism, clearly afterlife faith plays important social roles: offering social cohesion around a common mythic worldview, offering sanctions for right living and thinking not only in this world, but also in the world to come.

The ways in which the afterlife is interpreted psychoanalytically are fairly well known. For the Freudian, it is, one way or another, a perpetuation in some corner of the consciousness of the Krishna-like infantile world of play and freedom, of its 'oceanic' consciousness exalted to the mystic's unceasing oneness with the Infinite, or of judgment by the omnipotent parent. For the Jungian, it may be the realm of the timeless archetypes, now become the heavenly Mother, Hero, and ever-reborn Marvelous Child. The devotee of romanticism, inclined to credit the world with more strangeness and wonder than appears on the surface, might see in myths and images of the afterlife, the ultimate frontiers of the Distant and the Past toward which his mind, enhanced by feeling and imagination, aspires in the quest for truth beyond the prosaic. On the other hand, those attuned to the pedagogical use of myth could hardly overlook the teaching value of visions of the afterlife that reinforce proper doctrines and morals.

Yet, although afterlife myth and image can be approached critically from several points of view, and no doubt should be, that is not to assume that translating myths old and new into the language of a contemporary psychological or social scientific discipline is necessarily the last word. The human mind is an endlessly complex maze, and has ways of getting itself out of most of the traps it gets itself into. More questions can be asked, and stories told, about the meaning and backstory of human consciousness on this planet than have easy or complete answers. We must leave it that myths and images of the afterlife are tales in which we have endeavored both to ask and to answer the questions.

Further Reading

Please note that books in the area of mythology of the afterlife are very numerous; the following can only be considered a small sampling.

General

Coward, Harold, *Life After Death in World Religions*. Maryknoll, NY: Orbis Books, 1997.

Frazer, James G., *The Belief in Immortality* (3rd edn). London: Macmillan, 1924.

Holck, Frederick H., ed., *Death and Eastern Thought*. Nashville, TN: Abingdon Press, 1974.

Lewis, James R., *Encyclopedia of Afterlife Beliefs and Phenomena*. Detroit, MI: Gale Research, 1994.

MacGregor, Geddes, *Images of Afterlife*. New York: Paragon House, 1992.

Obayashi, Hiroshi, ed., *Death and Afterlife: Perspectives of World Religions*. Westport, CT: Greenwood Press, 1992.

Obeyesekere, Ganbanath, *Imagining Karma: Ethical Transformations in Amerindian, Buddhist, and Greek Rebirth*. Berkeley, CA: University of California Press, 2002.

Sullivan, Lawrence, ed., *Death, Afterlife and the Soul: Selections from the Encyclopedia of Religion*, Mircea Eliade, Editor in Chief. New York: Macmillan, and London: Collier Macmillan, 1987, 1989.

Taylor, Richard P., *Death and the Afterlife: A Cultural Encyclopedia*. Santa Barbara, CA: ABC-CLIO, 2000.

Primal Religions

Benson, Elizabeth P., ed., *Death and the Afterlife in Pre-Columbian America*. Washington, DC: Dumbarton Oaks Research Library, 1975.

Bockie, Simon, *Death and the Invisible Powers: The World of Kongo Belief*. Bloomington, IN: Indiana University Press, 1993.

Eliade, Mircea, *Shamanism: Archaic Techniques of Ecstasy*. Trans. William R. Trask. New York: Pantheon Books, 1964.

Leeming, David Adams and Jake Page, *The Mythology of Native North America*. Norman: University of Oklahoma Press, 1998.

Yamada, Takako, *The World View of the Ainu*. London: Kegan Paul, 2001.

Ancient Religions

Davidson, H. R. Ellis, *The Road to Hel: A Study of the Conception of the Dead in Old Norse Literature*. New York: Greenwood, 1968 (1st pub. 1943).

Hope, Valerie M., *Death in Ancient Rome: A Sourcebook*. London and New York: Routledge, 2007.

Macchioro, Vittorio, *From Orpheus to Paul*. New York: Henry Holt, 1930.

Mitchell, Stephen, *Gilgamesh: A New English Version*. New York: Free Press, 2004.

Sourvinou-Inwood, Christine, *'Reading' Greek Death: To the End of the Classical Period*. Oxford: Clarendon Press; New York: Oxford University Press, 1996.

Spencer, A. J., *Death in Ancient Egypt*. Harmondsworth: Penguin, 1982.

Hinduism

Deutsch, Eliot, *Advaita Vedanta: A Philosophical Reconstruction*. Honolulu: University of Hawai'i Press, 1969.

Eliade, Mircea, *Yoga: Immortality and Freedom* (2nd edn). Princeton, NJ: Princeton University Press, 1969.

Hopkins, Thomas, 'Hindu Views of Death and Afterlife,' in Hiroshi Obayashi, ed., *Death and Afterlife: Perspectives of World Religions*. Westport, CT: Greenwood Press, 1992, pp. 149–64.

Jarrow, Rick, *Tales for the Dying: The Death Narratives of the Bhagavatam-Purāna*. Albany, NY: State University of New York Press, 2003.

Justice, Christopher, *Dying the Good Death: The Pilgrimage to Die in India's Holy City*. Albany, NY: State University of New York Press, 1997.

Kinsley, David R., *The Divine Player: A Study in Krsna Lila*. Delhi: Motilal Banarsidass, 1979.

Parry, Jonathan P., *Death in Banaras*. Cambridge and New York: Cambridge University Press, 2003.

Wilson, Liz, ed., *The Living and the Dead: Social Dimensions of Death in South Asian Religions*. Albany, NY: State University of New York Press, 2003.

Zimmer, Heinrich, *Philosophies of India*. New York: Bollengen Foudation, 1951.

Buddhism

Becker, Carl B., *Breaking the Circle: Death and the Afterlife in Buddhism*. Carbondale: Southern Illinois University Press, 1993.

Cuevas, Bryan J., *Travels in the Netherworld: Buddhist Popular Narratives of Death and the Afterlife in Tibet*. New York: Oxford University Press, 2008.

Cuevas, Bryan J. and Jacqueline I. Stone, *The Buddhist Dead: Practices, Discourses, Representations*. Honolulu: University of Hawai'i Press, 2007.

Gómez, Luis O., *The Land of Bliss: The Paradise of the Buddha of Measureless Light*. Honolulu: University of Hawai'i Press, 1996.

Matsunaga, Daigan and Alicia Matsunaga, *The Buddhist Concept of Hell*. New York: Philosophical Library, 1972.

Thurman, Robert S., Jr., *The Tibetan Book of the Dead*. New York: Bantam, 1993.

Chinese Religion

Bauer, Wolfgang, *China and the Search for Happiness*. Trans. Michael Shaw. New York: Seabury Press, 1976.

Jordan, David K., *Gods, Ghosts, and Ancestors*. Berkeley, CA: University of California Press, 1972.

Loewe, Michael, *Chinese Ideas of Life and Death*. London: Allen & Unwin, 1982.

Japanese Religion

Iwasaka, Michiko and Barre Toelken, *Ghosts and the Japanese: Cultural Experience in Japanese Death Legends*. Logan, UT: Utah State University Press, 1994.

Stone, Jacqueline I. and Mariko Namba Walter, eds. *Death and the Afterlife in Japanese Buddhism*. Honolulu: University of Hawai'i Press, 2008.

Unno, Taitetsu, trans., *Tannisho: A Shin Buddhist Classic*. Honolulu: Buddhist Study Center Press, 1996.

Judaism

Lamm, Maurice, *The Jewish Way in Death and Mourning*. New York: Jonathon David Publishing, 1969.

Raphael, Simcha Paull, *Jewish Views of the Afterlife*. Northvale, NJ: Jason Aronson, 1994.

Riemer, Jack, ed., *Jewish Reflections on Death*. New York: Schocken Books, 1974.

Ripsman, Dina Eylon, *Reincarnation in Jewish Mysticism and Gnosticism*. Lewiston, NY: The Edward Mellen Press, 2003.

Wexelman, David M. *The Jewish Concept of Reincarantion and Creation: Based on the Writings of Rabbi Chaim Vital*. Northvale, NJ: J. Aronson, 1999.

Christianity

Bernstein, Alan E., *The Formation of Hell*. Ithaca, NY: Cornell University Press, 1993.

Delumeau, Jean, *History of Paradise: The Garden of Eden in Myth and Tradition*. Trans. Matthew O'Connell. New York: Continuum, 1995.

LeGoff, Jacques, *The Birth of Purgatory*. Trans. Arthur Goldhammer. Chicago: University of Chicago Press, 1984.

McDannell, Colleen and Bernhard Lang, *Heaven: A History* (2nd edn). New Haven, CT: Yale University Press, 2001.

Islam

Eklund, R., *Between Death and Resurrection According to Islam*. Uppsala: Almquist and Wilksells, 1941.

Halevi, Leor, *Muhammad's Grace: Death Rites and the Making of Islamic Society*. New York: Columbia University Press, 2007.

Smith, Jane I. and Yvonne Yazbeck Haddad, *The Islamic Understanding of Death and Resurrection*. Albany: SUNY Press, 1981.

Contemporary Perspectives

Baym, Nina, ed., *Three Spiritualist Novels by Elizabeth Stuart Phelps*. Urbana and Chicago: University of Illinois Press, 2000.

Braude, Ann, *Radical Spirits: Spiritualism and Women's Rights in Nineteenth-Century America*. Boston: Beacon Press, 1989.

Ellwood, Gracia Fay, *The Uttermost Deep: The Challenge of Near-Death Experiences*. New York: Lantern Books, 2001.

Moody, Raymond, *Life After Life*. Atlanta: Mockingbird Books, 1975.

Santino, Jack, ed., *Halloween and Other Festivals of Life and Death*. Knoxville, TN: University of Tennessee Press, 1994.

Stevenson, Ian, *Twenty Cases Suggestive of Reincarnation*. Charlottesville: University Press of Virginia, 1974.

Swedenborg, Emanuel, *Heaven and Hell*. Trans. George F. Dole. West Chester, PA: Swedenborg Foundation, 2000.

Notes

1   Translations include Francesca Fremantle and Chogyam Trungpa, *The Tibetan Book of the Dead*. Berkeley and London: Shambhala, 1975; W. Y. Evans-Wentz, *The Tibetan Book of the Dead*. New York: Oxford University Press, 1927, 1960; and Robert A. Thurman, Jr., *The Tibetan Book of the Dead: The Great Book of Natural Liberation through Understanding in the Between*. New York: Bantam, 1993.

2   For further discussion of myth, see Robert Ellwood, *Myth: Key Concepts in Religion*. London and New York: Continuum, 2008.

3   William Butler Yeats, *Essays and Introductions*. New York: Macmillan, 1961, p. 107.

4   For the Axial Age see Chapter 6, and Ellwood, *Myth*, pp. 79–84.

5   C. G. Jung, 'The Meaning of Psychology for Modern Man,' in *Civilization in Transition: Collected Works of C. G. Jung X*. New York: Pantheon, 1964, pp. 148–9.

6   Karl Jaspers, *The Origin and Goal of History*. Trans. Michael Bullock. London: Routledge & Kegan Paul, 1953, pp. 1–27, 51–60. See also Ellwood, *Myth*, pp. 79–84.

7   Carol Zaleski, *Otherworld Journeys*. Trans. Carol Zaleski. New York: Oxford University Press, 1987, p. 29.

8   Ibid., p. 30.

9   Alice K, Turner, *The History of Hell*. Orlando, FL: Harcourt Brace, 1993, p. 100.

10 Colleen McDannell and Bernhard Lang, *Heaven: A History* (2nd edn). New Haven, CT: Yale University Press, 2001, pp. 100–1.

11 Aldous Huxley, *The Doors of Perception and Heaven and Hell*. New York: Harper & Row, 1963, pp. 63–4.

12 Nina Baym, ed., *Three Spiritualist Novels by Elizabeth Stuart Phelps*. Urbana and Chicago: University of Illinois Press, 2000. See also McDannell and Lang, *Heaven: A History*, pp. 264–73.

13   W. H. D. Rouse, trans., *The Odyssey*. New York: Mentor, 1937, pp. 124–5.

14   Stephen Mitchell, *Gilgamesh: A New English Version*. New York: Free Press, 2004, pp. 59–60.

15   Ibid.

16   Donald L. Philippi, trans., *Kojiki*. Tokyo: University of Tokyo Press, 1968, pp. 49–70.

17   Bojana Mojsov, *Osiris: Death and Afterlife of a God*. Oxford: Blackwell, 2005, pp. 88–9.

18   A. J. Spencer, *Death in Ancient Egypt*. Harmondsworth: Penguin, 1982.

19   Hugh G. Evelyn-White, trans., *Hesiod*. Cambridge, MA: Harvard University Press, 1964, p. 95.

20   H. R. Ellis Davidson, *The Road to Hel: A Study of the Conception of the Dead in Old Norse Literature*. New York: Greenwood, 1968, pp. 85–90.

21   Manfred Clauss, *The Roman Cult of Mithras*. Trans. Richard Gordon. New York: Routledge, 2000, pp. 81–4. See also Roger L. Beck, *The Cult of Mithras in the Roman Empire: Mysteries of the Unconquered Sun*. New York: Oxford University Press, 2005.

22   However, the distinguished scholar of Zoroastrianism Mary Boyce, in *Zoroastrians: Their Beliefs and Practices* (London: Routledge & Kegan Paul, 1979, p. 18), dates Zarathustra as early as 1700–1500 B.C.E., basing her conjecture on the archaic language of the Gathas or hymns ascribed to the prophet himself, and the Neolithic cultural world in which he seemed to dwell.

23   Piloo Nanavutty, *The Gathas of Zarathustra*. Ahmendabad: Mapin, 1999, p. 92.

24   Mary Boyce, *Zoroastrians*, pp. 27–9.

25   Swami Prabhavananda and Frederick Manchester, trans., *The Upanishads: Breath of the Eternal*. Hollywood, CA: Vedanta Press, 1947, 1983, p. 20. Some of the discussion of the Katha Upanishads is adapted from Robert S. Ellwood and Barbara McGraw, *Many Peoples, Many Faiths*. Upper Saddle River, NJ: Prentice Hall, 2009, pp. 62–3.

26   Ibid.

27   Ibid., p. 22.

28   Prabhavananda and Manchester, *Upanishads*, pp. 27–8.

29   See Laurence G. Thompson, *Chinese Religion: An Introduction*. Encino, CA: Dickenson, 1975, p. 10.

30   Emily M. Ahern, *The Cult of the Dead in a Chinese Village*. Stanford, CA: Stanford University Press, 1973, pp. 91–2.

31   David K. Jordan, *Gods, Ghosts, and Ancestors*. Berkeley, CA: University of California Press, 1972, pp. 31–3.

32   David K. Jordan, *Gods, Ghosts, and Ancestors*, pp. 140–1. See also Philip Chesley Baity, *Religion in a Chinese Town*. Taipei: Chinese Association for Folklore, 1975, pp. 212–16.

33   Ruth Murray Underhill, *Red Man's Religion*. Chicago: University of Chicago Press, 1965, p. 79.

34   Andreas Lommel, *Shamanism: The Beginnings of Art*. Trans. Michael Bullock. New York: McGraw-Hill, 1967, p. 97. See also Jay Miller, *Shamanic Odyssey: The Lushootseed Salish Journey to the Land of the Dead*. Menlo Park, CA: Ballena Press, 1988, especially pp. 21–50 with first-hand accounts of various observers.

35   H. B. Alexander, *North American Mythology*. Boston: Marshall Jones, 1916, pp. 147–9.

36   Vittorio Macchioro, *From Orpheus to Paul*. New York: Henry Holt, 1930, p. 33.

37   Takako Yamada, *The World View of the Ainu*. London: Kegan Paul, 2001, pp. 32–5.

38   James L. Brain, 'Ancestors as Elders in Africa – Further Thoughts,' *Africa* XLIII, no. 2 (April 1973), p. 130.

39   W. D. Hammond-Tooke, *Boundaries and Belief: The Structure of a Sotho Worldview*. Johannesburg: Witwatersrand University Press, 1981, pp. 86–7.

40   Matthew Cooper, 'Langalanga Religion,' *Oceania* XLIII, no. 2 (December 1972), pp. 113–22.

41   James G. Frazer, *The Belief in Immortality* (3rd edn). London: Macmillan, 1924, pp. 165–9.

42   William Lynwood Montell, *Ghosts Across Kentucky*. Lexington: University Press of Kentucky, 2000, p. 8.

43   Richard Stoneman, *The Greek Alexander Romance*. London and New York: Penguin Books, 1991, pp. 120–3.

44   P. Sims-Williams, 'The Early Welsh Arthurian Poems,' in Rachel Bromwich, A. O. H. Bronwich, and Brynley F. Roberts, eds., *The Arthur of the Welsh: The Arthurian Legend in Medieval Welsh Literature*. Cardiff: University of Wales Press, 1991, pp. 33–71.

45   *Mail Online*, Oct. 3, 2009. http://www.dailymail.co.uk/sciencetech/article-121.

46   Cited Wolfgang Bauer, *China and the Search for Happiness*. Trans. Michael Shaw. New York: Seabury press, 1976, pp. 95–6.

47   *The Upanishads: Breath of the Eternal.* Trans. Swami Prabha-
      vananda and Frederick Manchester. Hollywood, CA: Vedanta
      Press, 1947. 1983 ed., pp. 176–7.

48   Ibid., pp. 177–8.

49   Ibid., p. 24.

50   Ibid., pp. 170–1.

51   Ibid., p. 178.

52   *The Laws of Manu.* Trans. G. Bühler. Delhi: Motilal Banarsidass,
      1964 (1st pub. Oxford, 1886), p. 497. Vol. 25, *Sacred Books of
      the East*, ed. by F. Max Müller.

53   C. J. Ducasse, *The Belief in a Life After Death.* Springfield, IL:
      Charles C. Thomas, 1961, pp. 211–13.

54   The Harris Poll #90, Dec. 14, 2005. http://harrisinteractive.
      com/harris_poll.

55   Morey Bernstein, *The Search for Bridey Murphy.* New York:
      Doubleday, 1956.

56   Debunking views were presented in Milton V. Kline, ed., *A Scien-
      tific Report on 'The Search for Bridey Murphy.'* New York: Julian
      Press, 1956. For argument that the debunkers often jumped too
      quickly to unproven conclusions, see C. J. Ducasse, *The Belief in
      a Life After Death*, Chapter XXV, 'The Case of "The Search for
      Bridey Murphy," ' pp. 276–99.

57   Robert A. Baker, 'Hypnosis,' in Gordon Stein, ed., *The Encyclo-
      pedia of the Paranormal.* Amherst, NY: Prometheus Books, 1996,
      note p. 349.

58   Cited in David Stern, 'Afterlife: Jewish Concepts,' in Lindsay
      Jones, ed., *Encyclopedia of Religion* (2nd edn). Detroit, MI:
      Thompson Gale, 2005, I, p. 153.

59   On Merkabah mysticism see Gershom G. Scholem, *Major
      Trends in Jewish Mysticism.* New York: Schocken Books, 1941,
      1961, pp. 40–79.

60   Ibid., pp. 281–4.

61   Jacques Le Goff, *The Birth of Purgatory.* Trans. Arthur Gold-
      hammer. Chicago, IL: University of Chicago Press, 1984, p. 5.

62   Cyril Glassé, *The New Encyclopedia of Islam.* Walnut Creek,
      CA: AltaMira Press, rev. ed. 2001, *passim.*

63   Raymond A. Moody, Jr., *Life After Life.* Atlanta: Mockingbird
      Books, 1975, p. 48.

64   Cited in Philip Kapleau, ed., *The Wheel of Death: A Collection
      of Writings from Zen Buddhist and Other Sources on Death –
      Rebirth – Dying.* New York: Harper & Row, 1971, p. 50.

65   John Bunyan, *Pilgrim's Progress*. Chicago, IL: Moody Press, n.d. (Originally pub. 1678), p. 61.

66   Colleen McDannell & Bernhard Lang, *Heaven: A History* (2nd edn). New Haven, CT: Yale University Press, 2001, p. 59.

67   McDannell & Lang, *Heaven*, pp. 75–6.

68   Ibid., pp. 89–91.

69   Ibid., p. 93.

70   *Vita Nuova*, Trans. Mark Musa. New York: Oxford University Press, 1992, p. 36. See also Charles Williams, *The Figure of Beatrice: A Study of Dante*. London: Faber and Faber, 1943.

71   Ibid., p. 68.

72   W. H. Auden, 'Introduction to the Sonnets,' in William Shakespeare, *The Sonnets and Narrative Poems*, ed. by William Burto and Sylvan Barnet. New York: Alfred A. Knopf, 1992. Introduction by Auden (c) 1964. See also Reynolds Price, *Ardent Spirits*. New York: Scribner, 2009, p. 242.

73   McDannell & Lang, *Heaven*, p. 136.

74   Cited McDannell & Lang, *Heaven*, p. 148.

75   Letter to Hans, reproduced in Roland H. Bainton, *Here I Stand: A Life of Martin Luther*. New York and Nashville: Abingdon Press, 1950, p. 303. Comment to Magdalene cited in McDannell & Lang, *Heaven*, p. 153.

76   Calvin, *Institutes*, III, XXV, p. 273.

77   Emanuel Swedenborg, *The World of Spirits and Man's State After Death*. New York: Swedenborg Foundation, 1940. See also Signe Toksvig, *Emanuel Swedenborg, Scientist and Mystic*. New Haven, CT: Yale University Press, 1948.

78   Emanuel Swedenborg, *Heaven and Hell*. Trans. George F. Dole. West Chester, PA: Swedenborg Foundation, 2000, pp. 414, 418. Capitalization in original omitted.

79   Ibid., p. 313.

80   Lionel Giles, trans., *Taoist Teaching from the Book of Lieh Tzu*. London: John Murray, 1912, pp. 36–9.

81   James Hilton, *Lost Horizon*. London: Macmillan, 1933.

82   Edwin Bernbaum, *The Way to Shambhala*. Boston and London: Shambhala, 2001, p. 202.

83   *The Journal of George Fox*, ed. by John L. Nickalls. Cambridge: Cambridge University Press, 1952; Philadelphia: Religious Society of Friends, 1997, p. 27.

84   Thomas Traherne, *Centuries of Meditations*. Bertram Dobell, ed. New York: Cosimo Classics, 2007, p. 152.

85 David Lewis-Williams, *The Mind in the Cave*. New York: Thames and Hudson, 2002.

86 Stacy B. Schaefer, 'The Crossing of the Souls,' in Stacy B. Schaefer and Peter T. Furst, eds., *People of the Peyote*. Albuquerque: University of New Mexico Press, 1998, p. 138.

87 Aldous Huxley, *The Doors of Perception and Heaven and Hell*. New York: Harper & Row, 1954, 1990, pp. 53, 55.

88 William Blake, *The Marriage of Heaven and Hell*. Introduction and commentary by Sir Geoffrey Keynes. London and New York: Oxford University Press, 1975, p. xxii. This edition is beautifully enhanced by Blake's own illuminations in full color.

89 Bruce Feiler, *Learning to Bow: Inside the Heart of Japan*. New York: HarperCollins Perennial, 2004, pp. 121–2. See also Michiko Iwasaka and Barre Toelken, *Ghosts and the Japanese: Cultural Experience in Japanese Death Legends*. Logan, UT: Utah State University Press, 1994.

90 The source is a text from c. 800 C.E. called 'Transformation Text on Mu-lien Saving his Mother.' See Stephen F. Teiser, *The Ghost Festival in Medieval China*. Princeton, NJ: Princeton University Press, 1988, pp. 170–9.

91 J. M. C. Toynbee, *Death and Burial in the Roman World*. Ithaca, NY: Cornell University Press, 1971, pp. 62, 64.

92 Gerard Besson, *Folklore and Legends of Trinidad and Tobago*. Cascade: Paria, 2007.

93 For a remarkable documentary DVD, see Gael García Bernal, narrator, *La Santa Muerte*. North New Hope, MN: Dark Night Pictures, 2007. In Spanish with English subtitles.

94 Katherine Briggs, *The Vanishing People: Fairy Lore and Legends*. New York: Pantheon Books, chapter. 2, 'The Origin of Fairy Beliefs and Beliefs about Fairy Origins,' pp. 27–38. See also Lewis Spence, *British Fairy Origins*. London: Watts, 1946.

95 W. Y. Evans-Wentz, *The Fairy-Faith in Celtic Countries*. New Hyde Park, NY: University Books, 1966 (Originally pub. London, 1911), p. 169.

96 Ibid., pp. 71–2.

97 Y. Krishna Menon and Richard F. Allen, *The Pure Principle: An Introduction to the Philosophy of Shankara*. East Lansing, MI: Michigan State University Press, 1960, pp. 120–3.

98 Henry S. Olcott, *People from the Other World*. Rutland, VT: Charles E. Tuttle, 1972 (Originally pub. Hartford, CT, 1875), pp. 83–4.

99   Ibid., pp. 146–7.
100 Cited in Ann Braude, *Radical Spirits: Spiritualism and Women's Rights in Nineteenth-Century America*. Boston: Beacon Press, 1989, p. 64.
101 Hesiod, *Works and Days and Theogony*. Trans. Stanley Lombardo. Indianapolis, IN: Hackett, 1993, p. 28.
102 *The Odes of Pindar* (2nd edn). Trans. Richard Lattimore. Chicago, IL: University of Chicago Press, 1976, p. 7.
103 *Tibullus: Elegies* (3rd edn). Trans. Guy Lee. Leeds: Francis Cairns, 1990, p. 15.
104 *Cicero: De Re Publica, De Legibus*. Trans. Clinton Walker Keyes. Cambridge, MA: Harvard University Press, 1951, pp. 261–83.
105 Mircea Eliade, *Shamanism: Archaic Techniques of Ecstasy*. Trans. Willard R. Trask. New York: Pantheon Books, 1964, pp. 210–12.
106 Ibid., pp. 82, 84.
107 Cited Andreas Lommel, *Shamanism: The Beginnings of Art*. Trans. Michael Bullock. New York: McGraw-Hill, 1967, p. 29.
108 E. R. Dodds, *The Greeks and the Irrational*. Berkeley, CT: University of California Press, 1951; Vittorio D. Macchioro, *From Orpheus to Paul: A History of Orphism*. New York: Henry Holt, 1930.
109 Cited Macchioro, *From Orpheus to Paul*, p. 11.
110 Ibid., pp. 34–5.
111 See, e.g., Marvin Meyer, *The Ancient Mysteries: A Sourcebook*. Philadelphia: University of Pennsylvania Press, 1999, p. 101.
112 J. H. Chajes, *Between Worlds: Dybbuks, Exorcists, and Early Modern Judaism*. Philadelphia: University of Pennsylvania Press, 2003, p. 3.
113 Ibid., pp. 101–2.
114 I. E. S. Edwards, *The Pyramids of Egypt*. West Drayton: Penguin Books, 1947, pp. 27–8.
115 Nancy T. Ammerman, 'Golden Rule Christianity: Lived Religion in the American Mainstream,' in David Hall, ed., *Lived Religion in America*. Princeton, NJ: Princeton University Press, 1997, pp. 196–217.
116 *Bhagavad Gita: The Song of God*. Trans. Swami Prabhavananda and Christopher Isherwood. Hollywood, CA: Vedanta Press, 1944, 1987, p. 82.
117 Ibid., pp. 82–3.

118 Wilfred Cantwell Smith, *The Meaning and End of Religion*. New York: New American Library, 1964.

119 Henri Bergson, *Les deux sources de la morale et de la religion*. Paris: Alcan, 1932.

120 Evelyn Waugh, *Brideshead Revisited*. Boston: Little, Brown, 1945, p. 338.

121 From the *Tannisho*, a collection of sayings attributed to Shinran, collected by a disciple. Ryusaku Tsunoda, Wm. Theodore de Bary, and Donald Keene, *Sources of Japanese Tradition*. New York: Columbia University Press, 1958, p. 217; and Taitetsu Unno, trans., *Tannisho: A Shin Buddhist Classic*. Honolulu: Buddhist Study Center Press, 1996, pp. 5–6.

122 *How to Know God: The Yoga Aphorisms of Patanjali*. Trans. Swami Prabhavananda and Christopher Isherwood. Hollywood, CA: Vedanta Press, 1953; New York: New American Library, 1969.

123 Evelyn Underhill, *Mysticism*. London: Methuen, 1911.

124 St. John of the Cross, *Dark Night of the Soul*. Trans. E. Allison Peers. New York: Doubleday, 1959 (1st trans. Peers pub. 1933).

125 *The Life of Saint Teresa* [her autobiography], trans., J. M. Cohen. Harmondsworth: Penguin Books, 1957, p. 122.

126 Meister Eckhart, 'Blessed Are the Poor,' in Raymond Bernard Blakney, *Meister Eckhart: A Modern Translation*. New York: Harper & Brothers, 1941, pp. 228–9.

127 On Milarepa, see Lobsang P. Lhalungpa, trans., *The Life of Milarepa*. New York: Penguin, 1984, pp. 22–35.

128 *Life of Sri Ramakrishna, Compiled from Various Authentic Sources*. Calcutta: Advaita Ashrama, 1924, 1964, pp. 16–19. See also Christopher Isherwood, *Ramakrishna and his Disciples*. New York: Simon and Schuster, 1965, pp. 35–7.

129 Richard Heinberg, *Memories and Visions of Paradise*. Los Angeles: Jeremy Tarcher, 1989.

130 The twelve novels of the 'Left Behind' series, all published Wheaton, IL: Tyndale House, are (short titles): *Left Behind* (1995), *Tribulation Force* (1996), *Nicolae* (1997), *Soul Harvest* (1998), *Apollyon* (1999), *Assassins* (1999), *The Indwelling* (2000), *The Mark* (2000), *Desecration* (2001), *The Remnant* (2002), *Armageddon* (2003), and *Glorious Appearing* (2004), plus a sequel, *Kingdom* (2007), and three prequels, *The Rising* (2005), *The Regime* (2006), and *The Rapture* (2007), together

with various other spin-offs in the form of children's versions, interpretations, and the like.

131   Hal Lindsay, with C. C. Carlson, *The Late Great Planet Earth*. Grand Rapids, MI: Zondervan, 1970; New York, Bantam Books, 1973, p. 126.

132   Ibid., pp. 124–5.

133   Glenn W. Shuck, *Marks of the Beast: The Left Behind Novels and the Struggle for Evangelical Identity*. New York: New York University Press, 2005.

134   See Leonard L. Thompson, 'Mapping an Apocalyptic World,' in Jamie Scott and Paul Simpson Housley, *Sacred Spaces and Profane Spaces*. New York: Greenwood Press, 1991, pp. 115–27.

135   From 'In Memoriam,' *Tennyson: Poems and Plays*. Edited by T. Herbert Warren. London; Oxford University Press, 1971, p. 266.

136   Padmanabh S. Jaini, 'Stages in the Bodhisattva Career of the Tathāgāta Maitreya,' in Alan Sonenberg and Helen Hardacre, eds., *Maitreya: The Future Buddha*. Cambridge: Cambridge University Press, 1988, pp. 74–7.

137   Rory Mackenzie, *New Buddhist Movements in Thailand*. London and New York: Routledge, 2007, pp. 60–3. See also pp. 77–85 for background on millenarian movements in Thailand.

138   Manichaeism was founded by the prophet Mani (215–76 C.E.) in Iran, under Christian and Zoroastrian influence. Its complex doctrine emphasized radical warfare between spirit and matter, identified with light and darkness. The religion spread very widely under several forms from western Europe to China, where it had a distinct impact. See S. N. C. Lieu, *Manichaeism in the Later Roman Empire and Medieval China*. Manchester: Manchester University Press, 1985.

139   On the Eternal Mother motif, see Richard Shek and Tetsurō Noguchi, 'Eternal Mother Religion,' in Kwang-Ching Lu and Richard Shek, eds., *Heterodoxy in Late Imperial China*. Honolulu: University of Hawai'i Press, 2004, pp. 241–80; Susan Naquin, 'The Transmission of White Lotus Sectarianism in Late Imperial China,' in David Johnson, Andrew J. Nathan, and Evelyn S. Rawski, eds., *Popular Culture in Later Imperial China*. Berkeley, CT: University of California Press, 1985, pp. 255–91.

140   On the doctrine of the three successive worlds, see Daniel L. Overmyer, *Folk Buddhist Religion: Dissenting Sects in late Traditional China*. Cambridge, MA: Harvard University Press, 1976, p. 83; for an overview of the history see chapter 5 of the same work, 'An Outline History of the White Lotus Tradition,' pp. 73–108.

141   Jonathon D. Spence, *The Search for Modern China*. New York: W. W. Norton, 1999, pp. 112–13.

142   That case was made by Bernard ten Haar, *The White Lotus Teaching in Chinese Religious History*. Leiden: E. J. Brill, 1992. See also Nancy N. Chen, 'Healing Sects and Anti-Cult Campaigns,' in Daniel L. Overmyer, ed., *Religion in China Today*. Cambridge: Cambridge University Press, 2003, pp. 199–214.

143   Chen, 'Healing Sects,' ibid., p. 207.

144   Wm. Theodore de Bary, Wing-Tsit Chan, and Burton Watson, *Sources of Chinese Tradition*. New York: Columbia University Press, 1960, p. 639. See also Susan Naquin, *Millenarian Rebellion in China: The Eight Trigrams Uprising of 1813*. New Haven, CT: Yale University Press, 1976.

145   Thomas H. Reilly, *The Taiping Heavenly Kingdom*. Seattle: University of Washington Press, 2004. See de Bary, Chan, and Watson, *Sources of Chinese Tradition*, pp. 680–704 for Taiping documents.

146   *Kúrma Purāna*. Trans. Ganesh Vasudeo Tagare (*Ancient Indian Tradition and Mythology*, vols. 20–1). Delhi: Motilal Banarsidass, 1981, Part I, p. 241.

147   Hesiod, *Theogony and Works and Days*. Trans. Catherine M. Schlegel and Henry Weinfield. Ann Arbor: University of Michigan Press, 2006, pp. 60–2. The term 'Golden Age' was not actually used by Hesiod, though adopted by Virgil, Ovid, and other very influential later writers on the theme.

148   B. F. Skinner, *Walden Two*. New York: Macmillan, 1948. Excerpted in Gregory Claeys and Lyman Tower Sargent, eds., *The Utopia Reader*. New York: New York University Press, 1999, p. 380.

149   Friedrich Nietzsche, *The Gay Science*. Trans. Walter Kaufmann. New York: Random House, 1974, p. 273.

150   Ibid., pp. 273–4.

151   Cited Ned Lukacher, *Time-Fetishes: The Secret History of Eternal Recurrence*. Durham, NC: Duke University Press, 1998, p. 119.

152   Swami Prabhavananda and Christopher Isherwood, trans., *Shankara's Crest-Jewel of Discrimination*. New York: New American Library, 1970, pp. 90–3.

153   From Shankara's *Upadesasahasri*, a short popular work: Sengaku Mayeda, *A Thousand Teachings*. Tokyo: University of Tokyo Press, 1979, pp. 214–15; see discussion in Bradley J. Malkovsky, *The Role of Divine Grace in the Soteriology of Samkaracarya*. Leiden: Brill, 2001, pp. 74–5.

154   Cited in Lance E. Nelson, 'Krishna in Advaita Vedanta: The Supreme Brahman in Human Form,' in Edwin R. Bryant, ed., *Krishna: A Sourcebook*. Oxford and New York: Oxford University Press, 2007, p. 315.

155   Heinrich Zimmer, *Myths and Symbols in Indian Art and Civilization*. Edited by Joseph Campbell. New York: Pantheon Books, 1946, pp. 195–6.

156   Jadunath Sinha, 'Bhagavata Religion: The Cult of Bhakti,' in Haridas Bhattacharyya, ed., *The Cultural Heritage of India*. Calcutta: The Ramakrishna Mission Institute of Culture, 1956, vol. 4, pp. 152–6.

157   From the *Vedarthasmgraha*; cited and translated in John Breasted Carman, *The Theology of Ramanuja*. New Haven, CT: Yale University Press, 1974, p. 170.

158   *The Wisdom of God (Srimad Bhagavatam)*. Trans. Swami Prabhavananda. New York: Capricorn Books, 1968, pp. 199–200.

159   Edwin F. Bryant, trans., *Krishna: The Beautiful Legend of God: Śrīmad Bhāgavata Purana, Bk. X*. London: Penguin, 2003, p. 125.

160   David R. Kinsley, *The Sword and the Flute*. Berkeley, CT: University of California Press, 1975, p. 78. Diacritical marks eliminated and spelling anglicized. See also Kinsley, *The Divine Player: A Study in Krsna Lila*. Delhi: Motilal Banarsidass, 1979, especially pp. 112–19 on the Heavenly Vrindaban.

161   Farid Ud-Din Attar, *The Conference of the Birds*. Trans. Afkham Darbandi and Dick Davis. London: Penguin Books, 1984, pp. 219–20.

162   Cherry Gilchrist, *The Soul of Russia*. Edinburgh: Floris Books, 2008, pp. 99–100, 129–30; rev. ed. as *Russian Magic*. Wheaton, IL: Quest Books, 2009.

163   Robert Redfield, *Peasant Society and Culture*. Chicago, IL: University of Chicago Press, 1956, 1973, pp. 41 ff. See also Max Weber, *The Sociology of Religion*. Trans. Ephraim

Fishoff. Boston: Beacon Press, 1963, chapter 7, 'Castes, Estates, Classes, and Religion,' and Robert Ellwood, *Cycles of Faith*. Walnut Creek, CA: AltaMira Press, 2003, chapter 9, 'Folk Religion.' Parts of the present chapter are adaptations of this last reference.

164   Grey Gundaker, 'Halloween Imagery in Two Southern Settings,' in Jack Santino, ed., *Halloween and Other Festivals of Life and Death*. Knoxville, TN: University of Tennessee Press, 1994, pp. 247–66.

165   David K. Jordan, *Gods, Ghosts, and Ancestors: The Folk Religion of a Taiwanese Village*. Berkeley, CT: University of California Press, 1972, chapter. 13, 'The Underworld,' pp. 220–44.

166   See Emily M. Ahern, *The Cult of the Dead in a Chinese Village*. Stanford, CA: Stanford University Press, 1973, pp. 163–74, 216–19; David K. Jordan, *Gods, Ghosts, and Ancestors*, pp. 164–74, 220–44. See Cecelia Lai Wan Chan and Amy Yin Man Chow, eds., *Death, Dying and Bereavement: A Hong Kong Experience*. Hong Kong: Hong Kong University Press, 2006, especially chapter. 4, Peter Ka Hing Cheung, Cecelia Lai Wan Cahn, Wai Fu, Yawen Li and Grace Yee Kam Pauy Cheung, ' "Letting Go" and "Holding On": Grieving and Traditional Death Rituals in Hong Kong,' and chapter. 5, Chi Tim Lai, 'Making Peace with the Unknown: A Reflection of Daoist Funcrary Liturgy.' See also Francis L. K. Hsu, *Under the Ancestor's Shadow*. London: Routledge & Kegan Paul, 1949, pp. 154–65 for funerals; this work does not discuss the Taoist temple rites.

167   Adam Yuet Chau, *Miraculous Response: Doing Popular Religion in Contemporary China*. Stanford, CA: Stanford University Press, 2006, pp. 129–36.

168   Isaac Klein, *A Guide to Jewish Religious Practice*. New York: The Jewish Theological Seminary of America, 1979, pp. 279, 286; see also Maurice Lamm, *The Jewish Way in Death and Mourning*. New York: Jonathon David Publishing, 1969.

169   See Rochelle L. Millen, *Women, Burial, and Death in Jewish Law and Practice*. Waltham, MA: Brandeis University Press, 2004, for a critical discussion of the prohibition of woman saying Kaddish in Conservative and Orthodox Judaism.

170   See Jane I. Smith and Yvonne Yazbeck Haddad, *The Islamic Understanding of Death and Resurrection*. Albany, NY: SUNY

Press, 1981, p. 122, for the suffering of the soul in *barzakh* according to the deeds of earthly life.

171 Leor Halevi, *Muhammad's Grave: Death Rites and the Making of Islamic Society*. New York: Columbia University Press, 2007, pp. 197–205. See also R. Eklund, *Between Death and Resurrection According to Islam*. Uppsala: Almquist and Wilksells, 1941.

172 Thomas G. Long, 'The Good Funeral,' *The Christian Century*, Oct. 6, 2009, p. 21.

173 Harvey Green, *The Light of the Home*. New York: Pantheon Books, 1983, pp. 167–80; Judith Flanders, *Inside the Victorian Home*. New York: W. W. Norton, 2004, pp. 369–89; Sally Mitchell, *Daily Life in Victorian England*. Westport, CT: Greenwood Press, 1996, pp. 160–3.

174 Long, 'Good Funeral,' p. 20.

175 Jackqueline S. Thursby, *Funeral Festivals in America*. Lexington, KY: University Press of Kentucky, 2006, pp. 136–7.

176 Pew forum on Religion and Public Life, *U. S. Religious Landscape Survey*, 2009, http://religions.pewforum.org/reports, p. 11.

177 Robert Ellwood, *Myth: Key Concepts in Religion*. London and New York: Continuum, 2008.

Index